"As a thirty-year officer in a large city police department, I can say that easy read that spells out what traumatized officers deal with in the aftermath of a critical incident. Step by step, Dr. Gallo provides practical exercises for officers to bounce back from trauma and to improve their performance at work, home, or wherever they are. The guidance is essential for any police officer wishing to understand trauma and its effects. I'll be sharing this must read with officers in my survival training classes."

— **Sgt. Robert K. Boehm**, officer survival, and defensive tactics instructor, SWAT commander, patrol supervisor, and union president

"In *Bouncing Back from Trauma*, Dr. Gallo has created a relatable and invaluable resource for police officers dealing with trauma or the broader consequences of exposure to critical incidents and human suffering. His approach is based on both his experiences as a police officer and professional training in acceptance and commitment therapy (ACT). Having delivered the Crosshairs approach in a large municipal police department both in training and treatment environments, I can attest to its effectiveness and relevance to police officers. The easy to follow strategies are also well suited as a self-directed guide.

— **Michael J. Craw, PhD, ABPP**, board certified in clinical psychology and police and public safety psychology from the American Board of Professional Psychology

"This is a wonderful book. It's written in the language of first responders. In other words, it's not written in psychobabble. Using this book, first responders will quickly learn what works when it comes to dealing with the trauma that they routinely encounter. Dr. Gallo's extensive experience in policing and working with uniformed service professionals has helped him craft a usable, dare I say "tactical" book filled with practical tools that any first responder will be able to use right away on the job and in their personal lives. This book is also a must read for practitioners in the business of helping first responders. The book offers wonderful insights into the lives of first responders and how they go about dealing with trauma."

— **Kevin Polk, PhD**, psychologist and creator of the ACT Matrix

"This is an exceptionally well-written workbook that can be used by first responders and emergency workers of all kinds to alleviate symptoms arising from exposure to trauma. The workbook is grounded in ACT and written in a style that is readily understandable. The workbook can be used independently as a stand alone, evidence-based approach to reducing and resolving these symptoms. As director of a psychological services bureau in a large metropolitan Sheriff's department, I highly recommend it."

— **Steven E. Sultan, PhD, ABPP**, board certified in police and public safety psychology from the American Board of Professional Psychology

Bouncing Back from Trauma

Bouncing Back from Trauma

THE ESSENTIAL STEP-BY-STEP GUIDE FOR POLICE READINESS

Frank J. Gallo PhD

Author's Note

All content found in this book, including text and images, is for informational and self-training purposes only. The content is not a substitute for professional medical or behavioral health advice, diagnosis, or treatment. If you decide to use the material, it does not imply a patient-doctor relationship. You should always seek the assistance of a medical or behavioral health professional with any questions you may have regarding a medical or behavioral health condition. Never disregard professional advice or delay in seeking it because of something you read in this book.

There is the possibility that errors were made while the information contained in this book was being prepared. There is also the possibility that changes have occurred in the behavioral health and medical sciences. Thus, the author does not guarantee that the information is correct or complete in every way. The author and any other party involved in preparing the material are not responsible for any errors or omissions or for the results obtained from using such information. You are encouraged to confirm the information contained in this book with other sources. The author is not responsible for the claims or content of materials accessed externally through a resource offered in this book.

Developmental editing by Jess Beebe, Waxwing Book Studio

Library of Congress Cataloging-in-Publication Data
Gallo, Frank J.
Bouncing Back from Trauma: The Essential Step-by-Step Guide for Police Readiness / Frank J. Gallo
ISBN-13: 9781546873204
ISBN-10: 1546873201
Library of Congress Control Number: 2017908548
CreateSpace Independent Publishing Platform
North Charleston, South Carolina

Contents

Exercises

Acknowledgments

To the many uniformed service professionals whom I've had the honor and privilege to learn from by listening to your trauma stories: without your trust and courage, this work would not have been possible.

Thanks to Bill Matthews for his support, mentoring, input, and friendship, all of which have been a valuable part of writing this book.

Thanks to Kirk Woodring for his support, mentoring, and friendship over the years and for giving me the first opportunity to work with uniformed service professionals in a clinical setting.

Thanks to Kevin Polk and Jerold Hambright for introducing me to the ACT Matrix.

Thanks to the many ACT practitioners and scholars whose ideas and scholarly work have contributed to writing this book.

Thanks to Kay Woodring for her helpful suggestions to improve my grammar and writing style in the first draft of this book. And thank you to Esther, Gloria, and Carolyn—the CreateSpace editing team—for their expert copy editing.

Thanks to my loving mother and father for their unwavering support over the years as I pursued what I want my life to be about.

Last but not least, a humongous thank-you to my wife and children for their love and support and for putting up with my long hours behind closed doors so that I could write.

Introduction

Welcome. I am grateful for the opportunity to share this book with you. I designed the book primarily for police officers struggling with painful thoughts and feelings related to a traumatic event that they have experienced. The training contained in the book is meant to help you bounce back, grow, and live life with more purpose and vitality, guided by what you care about (your values).

More broadly, other uniformed service professionals who have experienced trauma may use the book. What I mean by a uniformed service professional is someone who wears a uniform and is in the employ of a state or government agency. Law enforcement officers, military service members, firefighters, and rescue workers (paramedics and emergency medical technicians) are all uniformed service professionals. They work in operational settings that put them at risk of experiencing the full range of stress reactions to danger. Other trauma workers, such as emergency room nurses, doctors, mental health professionals, and disaster relief workers, may also use the book. I believe the book will help family members, friends, and mental health professionals provide a supportive environment in which you can recover.

I want to begin by thanking you for the chance to put my head on my pillow each night, close my eyes, go to sleep, and rest because I know that if something horrific were to happen, then there are men and women like you out there willing to help me without reservation. Thank you for all you do.

Now, I can only imagine what it's been like for you to experience a traumatic event. I appreciate your experiences, though, having thought about my own life story, such as witnessing extreme violence as a young child. In my police experience, some suspects punched me, kicked me, and spat at me while I arrested them. They held a knife, pointed it at me, or threatened others with it. Sometimes, they threatened to throw their feces, urine, and blood at me. I remember images of dead bodies, victims being stabbed, and the smell of death. In my mind's Rolodex of police work, there was also a suicide-by-cop call when I had to disarm someone holding a shotgun.

In this book, you'll find a practical and effective step-by-step training method to help you bounce back from a traumatic event and to make healthy changes in resiliency, work performance, and purposeful living. Over the years in using this training method with police officers and other uniformed service professionals, I've often heard them say things such as "I wish I'd had this training before this shit happened."

What is trauma? The word *trauma* is used to describe a broad range of situations that are emotionally painful and distressing. An event labeled as traumatic may involve a physical attack, firefight, serious car accident, or partner abuse. At work, seeing horrific pictures during an investigation may be traumatic. Even a routine medical procedure may be traumatic to someone. People's reactions to trauma vary quite a bit. Reactions can range from minor to severe disruptions that overwhelm someone's ability to cope and move on with living life. Traumatic experiences may happen to anyone. The possibility of something traumatic happening is even greater in settings such as policing. Later in training, you'll learn much more about trauma and how it may affect you.

For now, I'm guessing that you got this book because you've been trying really hard to make painful trauma-related thoughts and feelings go away, and you're expecting that the training in the book will cure, fix, manage, or get rid of that pain. Maybe you're expecting the training to be the gold-plated steam shovel that will lift and move your pain away. Well, the training that you'll go through is no gold-plated steam shovel. What's more, there are no magic medications to move your pain away permanently.

Now, you may keep doing what you've been doing, but you'll probably keep getting what you've always gotten. What you'll learn in this training is something else. You'll get to experience painful trauma-related thoughts and feelings in a way that frees you to engage in what life has to offer you in any situation. This way of working with your pain is grounded in Acceptance and Commitment Therapy (ACT).

What Is ACT?

ACT, which is pronounced like the word *act*, is an evidence-based therapy. That means it works for many people, and it may work for you. The reason we call the therapy ACT is because it focuses on learning by doing. However, ACT also mixes in other things, such as learning about your thoughts and feelings and what's important to you in life (Hayes, Strosahl, & Wilson, 1999, 2012).

During your training, you'll work on developing psychological flexibility. It's the ability to be more fully present, aware, and open to your experience in the current situation and to take action guided by your values (Harris, 2009; Hayes et al., 1999, 2012; Luoma, Hayes, & Walser, 2007).

A philosophy of science called functional contextualism is the foundation of ACT. It says that doing what's important to people involves defining what they do by whether it helps them accomplish their stated values-based goals (Hayes et al., 1999, 2012). In other words, functional contextualism is a way of talking about what's going to work for you. Are your thoughts and feelings helpful or unhelpful in doing what's important to you in the present situation?

On top of functional contextualism is relational frame theory, which is a theory of how human language influences experience and behavior (Hayes et al., 1999, 2012). It says that people use words to put things in various types of relations, such as comparing things: a nickel is smaller than a quarter. The moment they do that, some properties of that stuff automatically transfer from one to the other: a quarter is larger than a nickel.

So what's the problem? Consider this example. After being involved in a shooting at work, imagine that you think to yourself: *my life sucks. My life* is a huge network of experiences and behaviors. Some of the properties of *suck* may transfer across *my life* and its massive network. Everything you do now or later may seem to *suck.*

To keep the training practical, you'll use a simple and intuitive tool that I call the Crosshairs (Gallo, in press). It's a diagram adapted from the ACT Matrix that boils down the core processes of ACT into easy things to remember and do (Polk, 2011; see also Polk, Schoendorff, Webster, & Olaz, 2016). You'll use the Crosshairs diagram to look at situations in life that bring up painful trauma-related stuff like thoughts and feelings. Seeing through the Crosshairs, you'll learn to do five key things:

1. **Notice it:** Notice painful thoughts and feelings without getting caught up in them.
2. **Stay with it:** Stay with them because on the flip side are usually things you value.
3. **Let it go:** Let go of the habit of moving away from pain.
4. **Choose a direction:** Choose what you value in life.
5. **Just do it:** Take physical action in those chosen life directions.

Your Role in the Training

Doing the exercises in the training is a vital part of the ACT approach to bouncing back from trauma. Just like riding that first bicycle, the more you do it, the better you get at it. Another excellent outcome is that you tend to feel better. I remember teaching my son to ride his first bike. It involved giving him just a few directions. I asked him to sit on the seat, hold the handlebars, put his feet on the pedals, stay relaxed, feel how the bike leans left and right, stay upright, and pedal to keep moving.

The bike initially had training wheels on it to help my son balance the bike while riding. Despite the training wheels, he tipped over, fell, and hit the ground because he was stiff and scared. He scraped his knees and hands, bruised his elbows, and cried, but he got back on the bike to ride because it was important to him.

Eventually, I took the training wheels off as he got better at balancing the bike with practice. He learned to notice when he was leaning left or right and how to keep adjusting himself to stay upright. Then he rode faster and faster. In the end, he was jumping off curbs and riding through potholes because they stood in the way of where he wanted to go. Sometimes he fell and suffered an injury or cried a little—but then he got back on his bike and rode.

Learning by doing takes practice and may sometimes feel confusing. So don't expect smooth riding; take the words I say lightly, and let your experience guide you.

Traveling in a direction you value may look simple. However, it may bring up some painful thoughts and feelings along the way. You may think about them, take a detour by trying to ride around them, or even get lost sometimes. Noticing what's going on, opening up, and staying with painful thinking and feeling are key things you'll learn and practice because doing what's important is sometimes painful. It creates a sense of vulnerability because caring about things reveals what hurts you. You'll learn and practice skills to ride on any bumpy roads you experience along the way during the training. Also, at the end of the book, I provide you with some resources for professional help that you can investigate anytime.

Taking a step back, have you been caught up in fighting with painful trauma-related thoughts and feelings? Have you knocked them out permanently yet? Your role in the training is to let go of the fighting. If you haven't noticed yet, it's a losing battle in the long run, despite how natural it may feel in the short term. Fighting keeps you busy growing and pissing off the very pain monsters you've been trying to destroy over and over again. So in the presence of painful thoughts and feelings, you'll take action guided by your values instead. Who are you fighting with anyway?

Doing something new and different during the training may feel awkward and silly sometimes. Doing what it takes to live life with more purpose and vitality while having painful thoughts and feelings may lead your mind to tell you a few things during the training. It may say, *Ignore it. There's nothing new here for me to learn* (because you already know it). It may even say, *I need to change this a bit* (so that it feels better to you). Instead, keep a beginner's mind. Be open to experience what there is to experience because if you think you already know it, then there's probably little this training will offer you.

The Organization of the Book
The book is divided into seven training phases, most of which feature several experiential exercises and practices.

In training phase I, you'll learn how and why trauma may develop after exposure to a dangerous situation and how the nature of police work can worsen traumatic stress. Beyond the simple fact of frequent exposure to danger, police work involves values of toughness and separateness as well as requiring officers to reconcile their morals with the actions that may be required of them.

In training phase II, you are introduced to the Crosshairs diagram. You'll learn about the two axes (inner experiencing versus the outside world and avoidance versus approach), and you'll be introduced to the "Me Noticing" perspective.

In training phase III, you'll learn to map your experiences and responses on the Crosshairs diagram. You'll learn to notice painful thoughts and feelings, the actions you typically take to move away from pain, and the consequences and effectiveness (or ineffectiveness) of those solutions.

In training phase IV, you'll sharpen your present-moment awareness (i.e., noticing) skills by learning diaphragmatic breathing and increasing your awareness of bodily experiences. You'll learn grounding techniques that prepare you to reengage in valued living even in the face of unpleasant thoughts and feelings.

In training phase V, you'll learn to cultivate willingness. You'll engage in practices for staying with uncertainty, noticing impermanence, and riding out strong feelings. These skills serve as further preparation for living fully in spite of challenging internal experiences.

In training phase VI, you'll identify what matters most to you in life—including exploring how these things are often the flip side of the things you find most painful. You'll learn to step back from your thoughts, release your grip on long-held feelings and beliefs, and begin to take steps toward living the life you want.

In training phase VII, you'll choose an area of life for committed action, choose a value to guide your action, develop a values-based goal, and track your actions—and results—as you take steps toward valued living. The book concludes with a discussion of extending these practices, in all kinds of situations, for life.

Instructions for Guided Exercises

Many of the experiential activities in this book are guided exercises—at first. Eventually, you should be able to practice without a guide or a recording. For each guided exercise, you may do one or more of the following:

- Download the prerecorded exercise to your smartphone or computer, and listen to it as an audio file. Audio files are available for free at www.actforpolice.com.

- Record the exercise on your smartphone or computer so that you can listen to the instructions in your own voice.
- Have someone you trust read the exercise to you, or record the exercise in that person's voice.

When you read or record the guided exercises, you will notice three periods (...). The periods signal you to pause and practice what you're being asked to do. Give yourself five to ten seconds—longer if you want—to practice what's being asked of you. If you're listening to the downloaded audio files, then they already have pauses so that you can just practice.

Consider practicing first in a quiet and comfortable place where you'll be less distracted by noises and other things in the world outside of you. Keep in mind, though, that no matter where you practice, distractions inevitably show up—whether in the world inside of you, such as thoughts and feelings, or in the world outside of you, such as a phone ringing or your kids slamming a door shut. You can think of these distractions as opportunities to practice letting judgments about them pass by you, returning—again and again—to what you're practicing and being kind to your wandering mind because that's just what it does. Later in the book, you'll learn more about how to do these things.

Most of the guided exercises involve you sitting in a chair and practicing. However, I encourage you to practice in various positions, such as sitting on the floor; lying on your back, side, or stomach; standing; or even walking. The point is to practice in different positions you may inevitably find yourself in life so that the skill is available to help you live more fully—wherever you are and whatever situation and position you're in—guided by your values.

A Few Words before You Start

I will share with you some things about trauma that I've learned from personal experience, through formal education and training, as a former police officer, and from having the honor and privilege of listening as a psychologist to the life and work stories of many police officers and other uniformed service professionals. These individuals were willing to tell wholeheartedly what was on their minds to someone they thought deserved to be told. That's what I call *couraging*. It inspired me to write this book and to pay forward what I've learned. To ground our discussion and to illustrate key points, I use a fictional story about John. Here are some details I learned about John at admission for treatment.

John's story. John is a thirty-five-year-old married police officer admitted for treatment. He's been experiencing insomnia, dreams, and flashbacks following an officer-involved shooting at work. His wife noticed that he was reluctant to talk about what happened, so she let it go as a normal reaction.

John experiences intense emotions. He's easily angered and startled by noises and people passing by. He has difficulty sleeping and sometimes awakens at night from a nightmare in which he is reliving a firefight at work. John's wife became very concerned one day when he had a flashback while in the backyard: a car backfired, and he ran behind a tree seeking cover, thinking he was in the firefight again.

John's preoccupation with the shooting has become so intense that he is no longer interested in doing anything else. He is emotionally distant from his family. There are other important areas of his life, such as his health, in which he is no longer taking part because he spends a lot of time sleeping, staying home, and watching television.

Although fictional, John's story is a compilation of my personal and police experiences and work with police officers and other uniformed service professionals over time and across different settings. I have changed identifying information and combined details. However, John's story comes from truths of what I've learned over the years.

Put in a nutshell, what I've learned about trauma is that our trauma stories belong to us. They are part of us. They are not dangerous. They are important to have because in them are things we value. When we notice what matters to us in our stories, we feel less distress as we think about them. We can move in and out of our trauma stories, and despite their presence, we can still do what it takes to live our values. I am happy to share with you what I've learned in the service of helping you live the life you want to live before and after trauma.

TRAINING PHASE I:
Understanding Trauma

Human history tells a story of trauma. People fight wars, use weapons against one another, live through natural disasters, experience violence, and die. Generally, trauma is exposure to an event involving death or the threat of death, personal violence, or serious injury that is shocking and emotionally overwhelming. Traumatic events may be ordinary life experiences like these:

- Car accident
- Loss of a loved one
- Routine, invasive medical procedure

They may also involve extraordinary experiences:

- War or combat
- Terrorist attack
- Shooting
- Sexual assault
- Childhood abuse (physical or sexual)
- Physical attack or assault
- Fire
- Natural disaster, such as a hurricane, flood, tornado, or earthquake

Seeing or hearing about something horrible that happened to someone else may also be traumatic—for example, a police officer may be repeatedly exposed to details of child abuse. Even a child falling off a slide may be overwhelming and traumatic for some kids. Despite how careful people are in their lives, they may experience one or more life events as traumatic (Kessler et al., 2005). In policing, the chances of exposure are even greater. Many people think traumatic experiences are uncommon, but this is a myth.

The Effects of Trauma

Your responses to a traumatic life event are unique. No two people experience trauma exactly the same way. What may be traumatic and harmful over time to one person may be exciting to someone else. The point is that many things in your life history may influence how you respond to something you experience as traumatic. No matter how wide-ranging and complex your responses are, people have common reactions to a dangerous situation that later may be labeled a traumatic event.

Let's begin with the fact that a potentially dangerous or threatening situation signals the stress response. The strength of the signal depends on (1) the severity of the threat, (2) the possibility of the threat occurring if you take no protective action, and (3) the likelihood of your protective action working. A strong enough signal triggers normal protective stress responses to prepare you to fight with, flee from, or numb out the danger. You experience high stimulation of the sympathetic branch of your autonomic nervous system that activates the discharge of hormones like epinephrine to energize you to do your best.

Stress is your nervous system's natural accelerator. Stepping on the gas to do your best is a normal response to something dangerous, despite how abnormal or confusing it may feel. However, the stress response is a double-edged sword. Stress helps you raise your sword to do your best during the event. Too much stress can drag it down. When you press down on the gas pedal too hard, you may experience different high-stress reactions (Klinger, 2002).

Being in a Dangerous Situation

During something you experience as dangerous, you may have different thoughts and feelings:

- Disbelief
- Adrenaline rush
- Fear
- Horror
- Helplessness
- Anger
- Shut down

You may experience perceptual distortions:

- Tunnel vision
- Altered sounds (diminished, blunted, or intensified)
- Heightened visual details
- Time passing more slowly than usual (slow motion)

- Time moving more quickly than usual (fast motion)
- Disconnecting from your body and looking at the event happening from outside it—a protective response when your body secretes endorphins, a natural internal opium, to reduce the pain associated with a severe injury

In the Immediate Aftermath of Danger

Right after being involved in a dangerous situation, you may experience different things:

- Feeling numb or no longer having the ability to feel
- Feeling out of it or in a daze
- Feeling like the world is somehow different now and being disconnected from it
- Feeling like you're no longer yourself
- Forgetting details or important aspects of the situation
- Reacting physically, such as by crying or feeling nauseous

From Something Dangerous to Something Traumatic

During a dangerous situation, you may be busy doing what you trained to do. Later, when you begin to think about what happened, you may experience high-stress reactions. With opportunities to remember the dangerous situation and talk about it, for example, high-stress reactions become less intense, pass over time, and create only minor and temporary disruptions in most people's lives. Many people think everyone will need therapy after experiencing a dangerous situation, but this is a myth.

For some people, their high-stress reactions persist, worsen, and cause problems that significantly overwhelm their ability to move on with their lives. Such reactions can fall into four categories: intrusive, avoidant, cognitive/emotional, and anxious. A person needs to experience one or more intrusive items, one or more avoidant items, two or more negative thinking or feeling items, and two or more anxious items for over a month to qualify as being traumatized (American Psychiatric Association, 2013).

Intrusive Reactions

- Remembering the event (examples include images or thoughts)
- Dreaming of the event
- Acting like the event is happening again by responding to it and losing some sense of your surroundings, such as having a flashback
- Having feelings; hearing sounds; and seeing pictures, places, or people that remind you of the event
- Reacting physically to reminders of the event, such as sweating or your heart beating fast, which typically are protective responses to defend yourself against the memory

Avoidant Reactions

- Avoiding thoughts, feelings, or conversations associated with the event
- Avoiding activities, places, or people who remind you of the event

Negative Thinking or Feeling

- Exaggerating thoughts about yourself, others, or the world (e.g., *I'm a bad person; I can't trust anyone; the world is a dangerous place.*)
- Distorting beliefs about the cause or consequences of the event, leading to blaming yourself or others
- Forgetting parts of the event or having difficulty remembering it
- Experiencing fear, horror, anger, guilt, or shame
- Feeling no or little interest in doing things you used to do or would like to do
- Feeling disconnected or distant from others

Negative thoughts and feelings may lead to an absence of happiness, satisfaction, or loving feelings.

Anxious Reactive Behaviors

- Having difficulty falling or staying asleep or being restless during sleep
- Being more irritable than usual
- Being aggressive or bursting out in anger and then collapsing into numbness
- Having difficulty concentrating
- Looking out for threats more than usual, such as being hypervigilant
- Being startled easily by sudden noises or people coming up behind you

Since 1980, the American Psychiatric Association has recognized traumatic stress reactions as a medical condition. With help, though, people bounce back and return to living rich, full, and meaningful lives. You can too. There are treatments, self-help books, and training available, such as in this book. Many people think a posttraumatic stress injury such as PTSD is a life sentence—that once people experience it, they'll never recover—but this is a myth.

Being aware of the changes in you since experiencing a traumatic event is an essential part of the bouncing-back process. Understanding how your work may shape, maintain, and amplify traumatic stress is also important.

Police Work and Traumatic Stress

Police are a unique work group. Policing includes a set of behaviors, such as how to speak, what to do, how to dress, and how to see the world at work—and other things officers must do if they are to act comfortably and function effectively in their police roles.

Police officers learn distinctive ways of orienting to dangerous work conditions (Gallo, 2011). They subscribe to some fundamental beliefs developed on the job that are shown to work and that are transmitted to recruits (Gallo, 2008). The police organization accomplishes this through mechanisms such as training at the preservice and in-service levels. Particular beliefs about danger, morals, toughness, and separateness handed down through work experience and training may shape, maintain, and amplify traumatic stress.

Danger

Imagine for a moment that you pick up and read, listen to, or watch your favorite news source. There's a good chance that you'll hear or read something about a police officer being attacked during a car stop, at a call for police service, or in an ambush. Of course, you're aware that your occupation is a dangerous one in which there is some risk of harm due to what you do.

You learn at the recruit and in-service training levels to see your work as potentially dangerous. You learn to work in condition yellow, sensitive to the fact that whether you're on patrol or responding to a call for service, the situation may rapidly increase in danger. Today, combating terrorism reflects the changing nature of police work. The novelty, complexity, and uncertainty of acts of terrorism are risk multipliers in an already dangerous profession. Consequently, early in your career, you develop a worldview of danger that shapes training and operating procedures.

The paradox of danger is that actual harm to police officers doesn't happen a lot compared to the time they spend on the street or with citizens. When you're struggling with a memory of something traumatic that happened to you, a conditioned preoccupation with danger at work may lead you to generate absolute rules for how to operate. You go from thinking *people may want to harm me* to *people want to hurt me, and people may be armed and dangerous* to *people have weapons* or *the world may be dangerous* to *the world is a dangerous place*. Outside of work, for example, you may say, "I try to stay back at gatherings like cookouts. If I go to a restaurant, then I sit with my back to the wall and far away from everyone. If the place is busy, then I leave." Associating everyday harmless situations with danger activates needless defense responses quickly, excessively, and automatically.

When you're aware of the danger in life and uncertain about whether something is actually dangerous, it's like using a lighting-control dimmer switch. At work, you turn the dimmer switch up to brighten your surroundings when there is a greater potential for danger. Being able to see small changes in someone's behavior may help you stay alive. Turning the dimmer switch all the way up, though, may make it too bright—and blind you from seeing important things.

One of the potential pitfalls of traumatic stress is that you go from one extreme to another: being unaware or hypoaware (dimmer switch turned all the way down) to being superalert or hyperaware (dimmer switch turned all the way up). The fact is, you can use your awareness dimmer to change the brightness just enough to see what the situation calls for.

Morals

When work does present a life-threatening situation, police officers have the lawful authority to use force to defend themselves, protect others, prevent criminal behavior, and enforce laws. Using a firearm against another person or seeing such an event may bring to mind numerous moral challenges. This is especially the case for you as an individual in a social and work culture that fosters high moral and ethical codes of conduct about how things should work and how you should behave.

Police officers also have to make morally tough decisions sometimes during acute situations, particularly the choice to end life-sustaining treatment or to provide aid.

Even in light of training for the possibility of being unable to save someone or shooting someone and the person dying, you still face the need to resolve any morally inconsistent experiences you may have during and after such events. The real dangers of police work then create an additional risk of exposure to violating deeply held moral beliefs, such as what is right and wrong or good and bad.

When you're struggling with integrating into your experience an external event involving someone dying because of something you did or didn't do, you may sustain a moral injury. Trying to change your existing beliefs to make your behavior permissible in that situation may also result in a moral injury (Litz et al., 2009; Maguen et al., 2009, 2011; Nilsson et al., 2015). This lingering inner conflict may lead to chronic traumatic stress in response to feeling guilt (remorse about your behaviors) and shame (blaming yourself for what happened because of some personal flaw). It may also act as a reminder of your inability to do something. Eventually, you fear that your peers and others will judge you as weak.

Toughness

Police have long endorsed messages of being tough to get the job done, stay safe, and move forward. The work-selection process requires candidates to demonstrate some degree of physical, mental, and emotional toughness. You may have learned what it means to be tough by watching senior members model toughness. Media sources portraying tough cops are a source of learning.

Toughness is also tied to the traditional role of being male. In a male-oriented profession, toughness is a central component of the police character. For some females, this may add more pressure to measure up.

What is toughness? Character traits like being strong, aggressive, fearless, and courageous define toughness. Being tough, on the face of it, suggests invulnerability. Being tough is reinforcing. It actually helps you perform work activities that require physical, social, and psychological control. Police organizations also value its role in regulating certain feelings, such as feeling afraid during a dangerous situation. If you're to act comfortably, be accepted, and function effectively in your police role, then you must be tough enough.

Demonstrating outside-the-box behaviors to others, such as feeling afraid, sad, or even crying, may show weakness and suggest vulnerability. A possible consequence of perceived weakness is being called a wimp or wuss. Thinking that posttraumatic stress reactions are signs of a weak character can shatter your self-image of toughness and invulnerability. Stuck in trauma, you may separate from others and tough it out on your own to preserve strong police character and to shield normal human vulnerability. The alternative would be to admit perceived weakness by asking for help and then being judged, condemned, or rejected for it. You feel stuck and alone, and in silence, you miss opportunities to get help. Separating from others is something you may already be familiar with at work.

John's story. John told me once about responding to a call for service involving a neighbor dispute. When he arrived along with another officer, John noticed that the neighbors were talking in the street. As he walked calmly toward them, John remembered thinking, *I'm vulnerable. They'll think I'm weak. I'm not in control.* These thoughts triggered feelings of anxiety, worry, fear, and then anger. John yelled at the neighbors, "This is what you're gonna do," and then he grabbed one of them and walked him over to his car. John described his thinking, feeling, and acting as though he were going from zero to one hundred and back to zero within seconds. He felt overwhelmed. "I couldn't believe what happened. It scared me. I let the other officer handle the call, and I got out of there."

John sat in his car for a while, not knowing what to do and feeling guilty. "I shouldn't have grabbed that guy. I felt bad. I couldn't tell the other cop because he wouldn't understand, so I left. I called a buddy. He's a cop at another PD. I told him what happened. He got it. He knew. He's been involved in a shooting before."

Separateness

Isolation from others may stem from the way you learn to view your world at work: an us/them orientation. You learn to divide the world into categories: insiders (you and coworkers) and outsiders (everyone else). You create this worldview for a variety of functional reasons, such as solidarity, trust, cooperation, danger, group over individuality, or collectivism over individualism. To stay safe and to survive the work shift, you may see yourself as being different from the outsiders, whom you view with some suspicion. Naturally, people perceive things in group terms to simplify and make sense of their complex social worlds, including grouping people.

In trauma, you may even see yourself as being different from your nontraumatized work counterparts, as John did, and different from other important outsiders, including family members. Thinking *I'm different from them* and feeling separate makes it difficult for you to have relationships, interact with coworkers and members of other groups, and seek help.

Viewing the world and behaving differently at work, just as other professions do (an example is a lawyer seeing the world and its events as sources of potential litigation), helps you get the job done. However, what may be effective at work may not be as useful outside of it. For example, police officers patrol the streets, but you can't really do that at home. In trauma, maybe you're forgetting to take off the uniform as others do. You keep busy trying to stay safe all the time.

To help you see how a trauma memory in your head has taken control over what you do in your life, I'll introduce you to a tool I call the Crosshairs, which is coming up in the next phase of training.

TRAINING PHASE II:
The Crosshairs Diagram

At work, your department arms you with a variety of tools—such as a computer in the car, pepper spray, baton, and handgun—to do your job. As with these tools, the Crosshairs diagram is a simple and intuitive tool to help you at work and everywhere else in life. It's available to you as a picture on a piece of paper and always available to you as an image in your mind. In this phase of the training, we'll talk about what the Crosshairs diagram is and describe its different parts so that you can start using it.

Let's start by visualizing you giving a presentation to an audience at work. You ask the audience the following questions:

1. How many of you have experienced pain in your lives? What I mean by pain is have you ever found yourself thinking painful thoughts or feeling difficult feelings in life? If so, then raise your hand.
   What do your coworkers do? _____
   What do you do? _____
2. How many of you have ever struggled with or gotten caught up in that pain? If so, then raise your hand.
   What do your coworkers do? _____
   What do you do? _____
3. How many of you would like to struggle less with that pain? If so, then raise your hand.
   What do your coworkers do? _____
   What do you do? _____
4. Now, how many of you would like to live life with more purpose and vitality, guided by your values? If so, then raise your hand.
   What do your coworkers do? _____
   What do you do? _____

Look at how you think your colleagues responded. How did you respond? Whether you're in a room filled with five or one hundred people, what you would notice is everyone raising their hands if they are being honest with themselves. We're all in this together.

What exactly does the last item—living life with more purpose and vitality, guided by your values—mean? It involves struggling less with pain while doing more of what matters most to you. I call that valued living. Notice that I used "struggling less with pain," not "eliminating pain."

In this book, the training will arm you with a bottle of Windex and a roll of paper towels. It will bring you through an experience, inviting you to clean your window so that you can see your stuff. What you'll discover is that pain is a normal part of being human. Pain is not something to avoid, get rid of, or escape from. It's something worth having because you'll usually find things you care about on its flip side. To help you see this stuff, you'll use the Crosshairs diagram.

The Crosshairs Diagram

Imagine for a moment that you just washed some silverware and you're sorting it into a kitchen cabinet drawer. You can put forks, spoons, butter knives, and sharp knives into different piles according to their common characteristics. It turns out that you can do the same thing with situations in life.

The Crosshairs diagram is a highly effective tool to help you look at situations that show up in your life. Crosshairs, which you're probably familiar with, are intersecting lines in the shape of a cross. Binoculars, telescopes, cameras, microscopes, rifles, or guns may all use crosshairs for aiming at and focusing on a target of interest. Your targets of interest in this training are situations in life that bring up painful trauma-related stuff. However, you can use the Crosshairs diagram to look at any situation in life.

Did the situation occur in the past, is it taking place right now, or will it happen in the future? Whichever time you're looking at, putting the Crosshairs diagram on a life situation brings it into focus by dividing the situation into four parts. Part of the situation involves what you do in the world outside of you. Another part involves what you do in the world inside of you. There's a part that involves what you do to move away from any discomfort. There's also a part that involves what you do to move toward a valued life direction. You now have four parts in which to sort any life situation after noticing the differences and similarities between the parts. Using the Crosshairs diagram to divide and help sort this stuff results in being more aware of whether things you're doing to deal with painful trauma-related thoughts, feelings, and situations are helpful or unhelpful in living your values at work, at home, or in other important areas of life.

Before we begin the training, the first thing that we'll need to do, as with any police training, is to make sure that we're on the same page by using the same words to talk about things. Let's start with an illustration of the Crosshairs diagram as shown next. You may also watch an animated video that tells the story of the Crosshairs diagram. The video is available at www.actforpolice.com.

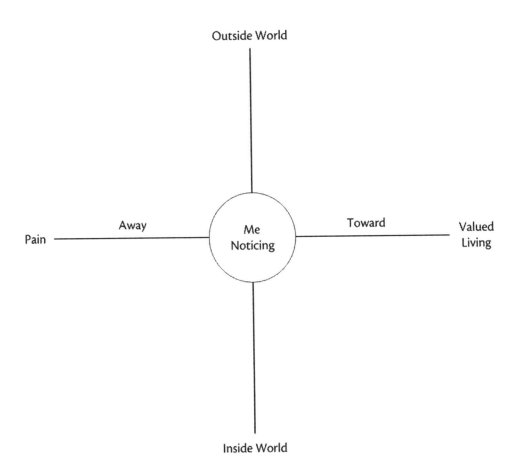

Before I begin describing the different parts of the Crosshairs diagram, let's identify the all-important context in which you find yourself acting in. Everything you do takes place in context. That is, what is the set of circumstances that form the particular situation for you to act in? Time is one aspect. Did the situation occur in the near or distant past? Is the situation taking place right now? Will the situation happen in the near or distant future? These three questions help you choose a time to map out a certain situation that you find yourself acting in.

Bits of information coming in through your senses—sight, hearing, taste, smell, and touch—are other aspects that make up the situation. As you read this book right now, what do you notice about the color of the page, the size of the text, and so on? By having "the situation" in your sights now, you can put the Crosshairs diagram on it to map out all the actions you do within it.

Outside World

What are you doing in the world outside of you? The outside world is made up of things you do with your body that other people would notice if they were present. In other words, if you were being recorded, what would the video show you doing with your arms, legs, and mouth? Maybe it shows you walking your dog, eating dinner, reading a book, and so forth.

Inside World

Thinking and feeling are also involved in what you do in the world outside of you. Thinking and feeling happen in the world inside of you where you're the only observer. What I mean by "thinking" is generating thoughts, images, and memories in your head. What I mean by "feeling" is having feelings, emotions, and sensations in your body. Saying "thoughts and feelings" is my code for all these things you do.

Location Line

Before moving on, turn your attention to the vertical line that connects your outer and inner worlds. This is the location line. It maps out the difference between the things you do that happen in the world outside of you and the things you do that happen in the world inside of you. When you do more things in the world inside of you, you might miss opportunities to interact with the world outside of you and vice versa. Even in light of those lost possibilities, you usually function well enough to get at least some things done.

For example, I remember driving my son to baseball practice, and my wife was with us. Now, I've driven him many times over the years to the same field for practice. However, on this day, we were running a little behind, and I drove right past the street. My wife was upset and said, "What are you doing? You missed the road. We're really late now!"

What happened? What was I doing? I was thinking. Caught up a bit in my inside world, I missed important information in my outside world to get me where I wanted to go. Now, the consequences weren't too bad, because I took the next street and got back on track. I wasn't too caught up in thinking, either, because if I were, I probably would have driven off the road.

Have you ever missed a street that you repeatedly traveled on to get where you wanted to go? What were you thinking? _____

_____

What were you feeling? _____

_____

How did your thinking and feeling affect your driving? _____

_____

Do you usually keep driving, or do you pull over and stop driving until you stop thinking and feeling? _____

_____

_____

When you're driving where you want to go in life, you won't find yourself doing things only in the world outside of you, because you need to use your mind to form thoughts and to speak (verbal behavior) so that you can interact with the outside world (Walser & Westrup, 2007). You also won't find yourself doing things only in the world inside of you. Let's look at a situation when John experienced a flashback.

> **John's story.** One day, John was walking in a building at work and suddenly smelled what he thought was gasoline. The smell triggered a memory of his police vehicle being hit by gunfire during a firefight. John felt overwhelming fear, his heart was pounding, and he was sweating. He walked to the end of the building's corridor, opened the door to the first-floor staircase, walked down the stairs, exited the door to go outside, and sat on a bench nearby. He lit a cigarette, smoked it, and eventually returned to work.

For John, even in those moments when he got caught up in his inner experience, he was still interacting with the world outside of him. John was walking in a building, sitting on a bench outside, and smoking a cigarette.

Valued Living

In the training, you'll explore ten areas of life to help you identify the people and things important to you. These areas are family, intimate relationships, parenting, friends, education, work, recreation, spirituality, community life, and health (Hayes et al., 1999, 2012). However, there may be more areas. You may also divide life differently than I have. For training purposes, we'll use these ten areas as a way to explore your living life with more purpose and vitality, guided by your values.

Pain

Pain is simply something unpleasant or unwanted that you try to avoid.

Purpose Line

The horizontal line that connects valued living and pain is called the purpose line. All the things you do in the world outside of you and in the world inside of you have some purpose to achieve some outcome, whether you're aware or unaware of that purpose. The purpose line maps out the difference between the things you do to move *away* from pain and the things you do to move *toward* valued living.

Toward actions involve having pleasant or wanted thoughts and feelings that you approach in living life guided by your values. Maybe you're thinking about *interacting with family enjoyably* (value). A physical move is watching a movie with them (goal). Feeling enjoyment and having a sense of satisfaction keeps these actions going. We'll talk more about values and goals later in the training.

Away actions involve experiencing unpleasant or unwanted thoughts and feelings that you try to avoid in living life. For example, you think *I'm broken* and feel sadness. A physical move may be drinking alcohol. Feeling better and experiencing a sense of relief keep these actions going. In the next phase of the training, we'll talk more about your away moves.

Over the course of living life, getting busy doing more things aimed at valued living results in less time available for those away moves. And working hard at trying to stay away from pain puts valued living on the shelf.

Using the location and purpose lines, you can now divide your trauma-related life situations into different parts. Everything above the purpose line involves actions you take in the world outside of you. Everything below it involves actions you take in the world inside of you. Everything to the right of the location line involves actions you take (inside and outside) aimed at moving toward valued living. Everything to the left of the location line involves actions you take (inside and outside) aimed at moving away from pain. You now have four parts in which to sort any life situation after you notice the differences and similarities between the parts.

Me Noticing

At this point, turn your attention to the center of the Crosshairs diagram. Now let me ask you this: Who can notice the situation you're in and all this stuff going on in the Crosshairs? If you said, "Me," then that's right. "Me Noticing" is at the center of the Crosshairs diagram because you're at the center of the point of view.

When you're looking at a situation from this position, it's as if you were a sportscaster calling a major football game on the radio. Two radio stations are broadcasting the game. However, station two symbolizes Me Noticing.

On station one, the sportscaster is calling the game from behind each quarterback. What does the game sound like to you?

_____

_____

_____

_____

You would probably hear the sportscaster running around, breathing heavily, yelling, maybe even swearing sometimes, and trying to avoid being tackled during the whole game.

On station two, the sportscaster is sitting high up in the stands where sportscasters usually sit and call the game. From this point of view, the sportscaster can see all the players on the field and tell you what's going on in the game.

Now, which sportscaster is giving you a very narrow view of the game? _____
Which radio station do you choose to listen to, and why?_____

_____

_____

_____

Me Noticing is the sportscaster on station two who is observing the game and giving the play-by-play commentary.

That said, just calling the game can get boring. At some point, you may choose to step out of the sportscaster booth and to get involved in the game. Maybe you want to sit in different seats closer to the field and to get involved from there. As you get closer to the field, what does the game feel like? Maybe there's anger or excitement. What do you do? Maybe you yell at the opposing team or you cheer on your team. You may even run all the way down onto the field and play the game of what you're thinking and feeling—and you don't have to.

Now that we've set up a common language to use, you may begin the next phase of the training. It involves drawing out the strategy you've been using to deal with any discomfort related to a past-trauma event that somehow has hijacked your life. You'll also investigate the consequences of using this strategy. This is a major step in healing a posttraumatic stress injury and training your Me Noticing ability.

TRAINING PHASE III:

Drawing Out Your Problem-Solving Approach to Pain

n this phase of the training, you'll discover how helpful it is to move away from painful thoughts, feelings, and situations related to a past trauma. You'll notice whether and how much what you've been doing is getting in the way of valued living.

Your Strategy

The first thing you'll need to do in investigating how pain is controlling what you've been doing in life is to write it out on a piece of paper so that you can see it. Writing it out involves listing your painful thoughts and feelings, listing what you do to move away from them, and then connecting how it all happens in living life.

Step One: List Painful Thoughts and Feelings

In the lower left part of the Crosshairs diagram that follows, write down the most frequent unpleasant or unwanted trauma-related thoughts and feelings that your mind and body generate in the world inside of you. We'll call this your pain list. Remember, thoughts may also be images and memories. Feelings may also be emotions and sensations. The following is a list of some all-time police unfavorites:

- Painful thoughts about yourself, such as *I'm weak* and *I'm not as strong as I used to be*
- Painful thoughts about others, such as *People will hurt me* and *I can't trust them*
- Painful thoughts about the world, such as *I'll never be safe* and *The world is dangerous*
- Painful thoughts about the event, such as *If only I had done something different*
- Painful thoughts about PTSD, such as *I'll never get over it* and *It's ruined my life*
- Painful feelings, such as anger, fear, guilt, worry, hopelessness, or helplessness
- Painful sensations, such as cold, jittery, paralyzed, empty, numb, sweaty, or hot
- Painful images, such as a muzzle blast, a dead body, or an abused child

Your pain list, as with others, is probably somewhat long. Life tends to add more items to the list—and even more when you experience something traumatic.

Step Two: List Things You Do to Move Away from Painful Thoughts and Feelings

When something painful for you shows up, it naturally, easily, and automatically triggers your mind to slip into a default mode of problem solving. Your mind begins to generate solutions to move away from the pain. The solutions it comes up with are supposed to get you to feel better, avoid or get rid of the pain, or escape from the painful situation—at least, you hope they will.

In the upper left part of the Crosshairs diagram, write down the most frequent things you do to move away from the unpleasant or unwanted thoughts and feelings you identified on your pain list. We'll call this your solutions list. Remember, these are the things a video would show you doing with your body to move away from pain. Maybe it's walking away, calling in sick to work, or drinking beer. Some all-time police favorites include the following:

- Eating junk food
- Lying in bed all day
- Watching television
- Drinking alcohol
- Using painkillers
- Working extra details
- Exercising more at the gym

As with the pain list, your solutions list may be quite long. As time passes, you'll probably add more solutions to the list, as others do, especially when you're just trying to get away from the pain of something horrible that happened in your life.

Step Three: Link Up Your Pain and Solutions

Now that you've listed items on your pain and solutions lists, you'll draw out your problem-solving approach to moving away from pain. However, before we begin, let's return to John's story and look at some ways that he tried to solve away his pain.

John's story. One day while eating lunch at an outside café, John thought, *I'm vulnerable to an attack*, and he felt frightened and overwhelmed (pain). He immediately got up from his chair and walked away from the café (solution), leaving his wife sitting alone at the table.

A couple of days later, John planned a trip to a home improvement store to buy some supplies for a new deck. While making a list of items to buy, he thought, *The store is a dangerous place. I can't go there; I'll never be safe* (pain). He felt shaky and anxious, and his heart began pounding (pain). John stayed home and watched television instead (solution).

The same day, John saw a movie on TV that showed a firefight. The movie triggered, in his head, images of muzzle blasts that happened during the firefight at work (pain). Upset, John walked away from the television to the kitchen and began eating pizza (solutions). However, he felt worse when he finished. He had a stomachache and felt depressed (pain). He decided to sleep it off (solution).

John woke up late the next day and missed his son's football game. He felt angry. Feeling and thinking *I'm angry* (pain), he yelled at his wife for letting him sleep too long (solution). Right after John yelled, he felt some immediate relief for just a few seconds before feeling guilty about yelling (pain).

In John's story, his solutions sometimes got him to feel better, to avoid or get rid of painful thoughts and feelings, and to escape a painful situation, but sometimes, they caused him more pain. Drawn in the following Crosshairs diagram is John's problem-solving approach to painful trauma-related situations that show up in life. The single arrowhead lines symbolize the links between items on his pain and solutions lists.

The Situation: PAINFUL LIFE SITUATIONS RELATED TO A SHOOTING AT WORK THAT HAPPENED A FEW MONTHS AGO.

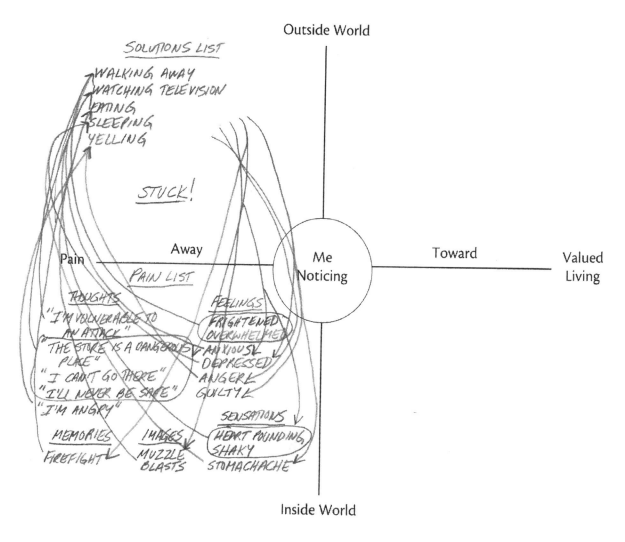

What do you see when you look at John's Crosshairs diagram? What John noticed is what we refer to as getting stuck. That is, doing the same thing over and over again and expecting that the pain will go away and never come back.

Let's shift gears now to drawing out your problem-solving approach to painful trauma-related situations that show up in life. Begin by choosing a thought on your pain list. Next, remember a situation when that painful thought came up. What did you do on your solutions list to move away from that thought? Draw a single arrowhead line from the painful thought pointing to the away move.

Later, in another situation, you noticed feeling an unpleasant or unwanted feeling on your pain list. Draw a single arrowhead line from your solutions list area pointing to that painful feeling. To move away from it, you returned to your all-time favorites. What did you do that time? Draw a single arrowhead line from the painful feeling pointing to the away move on your solutions list.

Maybe the same day or another day there was a situation in which you remembered an upsetting image or memory. Draw a single arrowhead line from your solutions list area pointing to that painful image or memory on your pain list. Disliking how you felt then, you returned to your solutions list and did something on it to try to get rid of that pain. What did you do then? Draw a single arrowhead line from the painful image or memory pointing to the away move.

Some of your solutions might be causing pain of their own. For example, John felt guilty after yelling at his wife. Remember a time when your solution made you feel worse, and draw that in the Crosshairs.

What about a time when a painful thought such as *I'm angry* showed up? Maybe you said something mean, broke something, or hit something to escape that painful situation. After you had done that, perhaps you felt some relief or felt worse. Draw that problem-solving approach to pain. You may also add thoughts and feelings together that led you to make an away move.

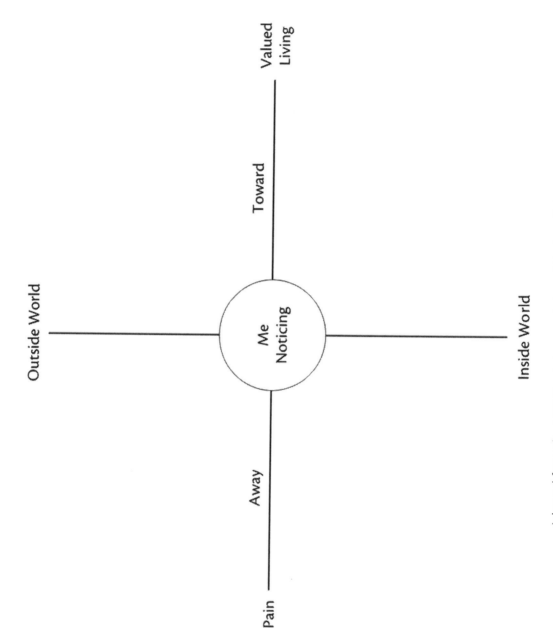

Adapted from the ACT Matrix by permission of Kevin Polk (2011)

Continue linking up more of your painful thoughts and feelings—including emotions, sensations, images, and memories—with the things you do to get away from them when they show up in situations. You may fill out another Crosshairs diagram if you want. When listing a memory, just label it with a word or two instead of listing all the painful thoughts and feelings that show up with it. As John and I demonstrated with his stuff, his memory of the firefight brought with it painful thoughts, feelings, sensations, and images. John could now say to himself, *Ah, there's that firefight.*

The Consequences of Trying to Problem Solve Pain

What do you see when you look at your Crosshairs diagram and the links between your painful thoughts and feelings and the things you do to move away from them? From my personal experience and in working with police officers struggling with a traumatic memory, I'm guessing that you're looking at a pattern of being stuck, just as John did.

You get stuck because your pattern of behavior comes under the control of painful thoughts and feelings. When pain shows up, you come up with a solution to move away from it. This is the way things usually happen. You strengthen this pattern of behavior each time you do something that moves you away from pain, gets you to feel good, gets you to avoid or get rid of that pain, or gets you to escape from that painful situation. The chance of you making an away move again when pain shows up in a situation is pretty good. So your mind keeps on bullying you, telling you what to do, and insisting you go along for the ride. What begins as solutions serving you now seems to become habits that require you serving them.

In any situation, treating whatever painful stuff shows up as a problem to be solved is natural. There is an evolutionary benefit to figuring out a solution to fight with, flee from, or numb out something your mind thinks is dangerous. Maybe you learned in the academy or in-service training to be tough, strong, and invulnerable, putting on your emotional body armor to shield yourself from feeling unpleasant feelings. Maybe you learned from peers at work to move away from pain by doing things like drinking alcohol. Going out and drinking after a tough shift at work reinforces using alcohol as a social and mental approach to dealing with job stressors and surviving the work shift.

Maybe someone in life told you that you're supposed to feel happy and not sad. Perhaps you learned from books about how to escape from or control things your mind tells you are painful. Besides, when you repeatedly fix broken things, such as a flat tire, or get rid of broken things, such as a watch, it makes sense to use the same problem-solving approach to deal with painful things that show up inside of you.

How is relating to your pain using the problem-solving approach working for you? _____

_____

_____

How long have you been having painful thoughts and feelings related to your traumatic experi-ence? _____

_____

_____

How long have you been doing things to move away from them? _____

_____

_____

Have any of your solutions permanently stopped your painful trauma-related thinking and feeling? How about stopping your painful thinking and feeling in life? _____

_____

_____

What are you no longer doing that you used to do before the traumatic event happened?

_____

_____

_____

_____

_____

Exercise: Figuring Out Valued Living

In this exercise inspired by ideas from the Values Compass activity (Dahl, Plumb, Stewart, & Lundgren, 2009), you'll investigate the consequences of using the problem-solving approach to try to make pain go away. You'll figure out how important different areas of life are, such as family and friends, and how much you've been doing in these areas lately, such as having dinner with your wife and kids or playing basketball with your buddies. You'll also figure out whether you're doing much less or much more than you used to do before the traumatic event happened. Your answers to the following questions will help you later in the training to develop an action plan to live life guided by your values:

1. Look at the different areas of life on the illustration that follows.
2. Begin with the box labeled "I" that stands for importance. Using a scale from 0 (not very important) to 10 (very important), write down how important, right now, this area of life is

to you. You may have the same ratings for different areas of life (e.g., Family = 10 and Friends = 10), so don't rank them in order, such as 1, 2, and 3.

3. Go to the box labeled "B" that stands for behavior. Using a scale from 0 (not doing very much) to 10 (doing a lot), write down how much, over the past six months, you've been doing in each area of life. You may have the same ratings for different areas of life, so don't rank them in order.

4. Do the following subtraction problem for each area of life, and write your answer in the box labeled "A" that stands for answer: I – B = A. Then circle either the plus symbol for a positive answer or the minus symbol for a negative answer. Circle neither if the answer equals zero. Here are some examples:

   ▪ Positive answer: 10 ("I" value for Family) 5 ("B" value for Family) = +5
   ▪ Negative answer: 7 ("I" value for Friends) 10 ("B" value for Friends) = –3
   ▪ Zero answer: 10 ("I" value for Health) 10 ("B" value for Health) = 0

Figuring Out Valued Living

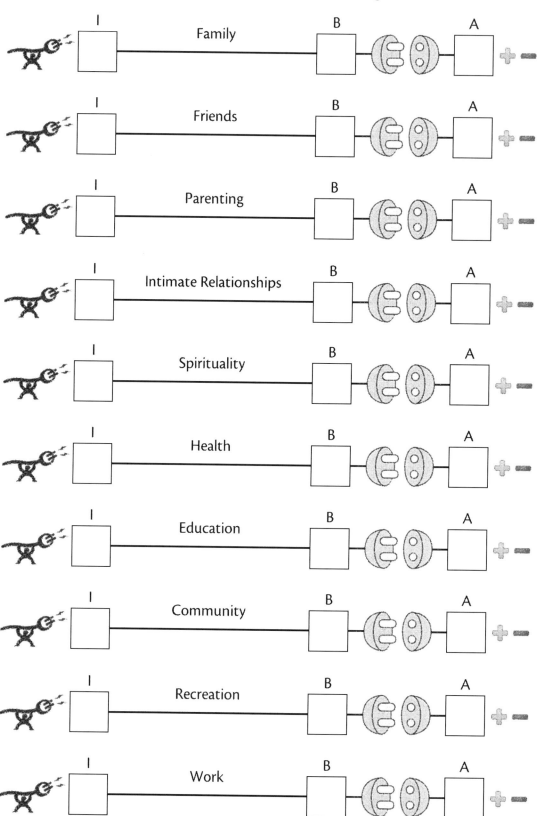

Next, look at your importance ratings in the "I" boxes. Here are some ways to understand how you came up with your numbers:

- High numbers may indicate that when you've done things that matter to you in this area of life, you've had pleasant experiences over and over again.
- A low number may mean that you've had a lot of painful experiences and fewer pleasant ones in this area of life.
- A low number may mean that you've had little to no experience in this area of life as a source of having pleasant experiences. For example, you may not value parenting at all if you're single with no kids and define parenting as having a child.
- Another possible reason for a low number is that you neither like nor dislike this area of life. You're just doing things for others who matter to you. For example, maybe it's doing community stuff with your best friend because your friend likes it. It's always possible, though, that the stuff becomes a source of pleasant experiences for you, and you value community too.

Now look at your answers in the "A" boxes. Here are some ways to understand and use those numbers to live with more purpose and vitality according to your values:

- A zero value means you're putting as much effort into this area of life as you value it.
- A positive number indicates that this is an area of life in which to do more things. The plus symbol stands for adding activities.
- A negative number suggests that this is an area of life in which to do fewer things. The minus symbol means to subtract activities because there's a good chance of burnout, resentment, greater distress, or a growing sense of meaninglessness over time when you're putting much effort into something you don't value very much.

When looking at your numbers, it's important to remember that you're a historical being. To every life situation, you bring with you a rich history of behaviors. To complete this exercise, you recollected your experiences to generate the numbers. The meanings of your answers in the "A" boxes are significantly influenced by how you came to rate the importance of each area of life ("I" boxes), which you may change over time.

When you're busy living life on the left side of the Crosshairs, you're putting valued living on the shelf. Relating to pain the same old way over time, you lose touch with what's important to you. The more you strengthen your habitual pattern of away moves, the more afraid you become to go into what brings you unpleasantness and the more quickly you become irritated by painful thoughts, feelings, and situations. You become thin-skinned, easily provoked into doing the same old familiar thing to try to move away from pain. You create a future in which you're less able to stay with the pain that shows up in life, and the conditions for valued living come along less often.

John's story. After completing the Figuring Out Valued Living exercise, John noticed that he rated the importance of work a 2 and behavior a 10. The difference equaled 8, which suggested that he was putting more effort into work than he valued it. Therefore, John should decrease working or do fewer things at work. Now, it may be that work became another solution. However, for John, work became a source of total bullshit: administrative, legal, union, political, hurtful, and touchy-feely crap. John's bullshit list grew quite long. He developed growing anger, frustration, irritability, and intolerance to things at work. Thinking everything was bullshit allowed John to explain, deal with, and move away from painful work-related thoughts and feelings, such as calling in sick to work. John no longer saw any value in work, thus his low importance rating.

Living life on the left side of the Crosshairs diagram is like playing the Whac-A-Mole game all day and every day. Is it hopeless? Using the problem-solving approach to move away from pain is hopeless in the long run. It's hopeless when it doesn't work and brings you more pain. It's hopeless when the consequences are that you're no longer living your values.

Are you hopeless? No! It's not you who is broken. It's not you who is defective. It's not you who needs fixing. It's the problem-solving approach to pain that you've been using. It doesn't work, and it's not your fault. You've been doing what you're hardwired to do and what you've learned from others. Getting stuck in it is optional.

All that said, you may choose to keep doing what you've always done, and you'll probably get what you've always gotten. Yes, you may choose a problem-solving way of relating to reports about painful thoughts and feelings that your mind and body generate and send you all the time, but you don't have to. Your job is to take some reports seriously and respond to them. The other reports you can just file in your memory, appreciate, and thank your mind and body for the hard work they're doing for you. It's like being the chief of police. You have a staff of commanders. They create and send you reports about how the police department is doing. Now, you can't act on every report, so you act on some of them, and the others you store in a folder on your computer's hard drive.

Are you willing now to begin doing something different, driving in a different direction, and taking your mind and body along for the ride instead of you being the passenger? Doing something else that moves you toward valued living begins with building a foundation from which to engage living your values. You'll work on this in the next phase of the training.

Before we end here with some practice to do between training sessions, be sure to keep your filled-in Crosshairs diagram and the Figuring Out Valued Living worksheet so that you have them available for other exercises later in the training.

What Can You Do Now to Practice?

Take a break now from the training so that you can complete the action plan given next. Give yourself enough time—a few days or more—to complete it before you begin the next training session.

1. Notice when painful trauma-related thoughts and feelings show up in a particular situation.
2. Notice whether you do anything to move away from them.
3. Use the Crosshairs diagram to draw what happens in the situation. Remember to describe the situation you're in first, and then put the Crosshairs diagram on it so that you can map out all the actions you do within it.

The Situation:

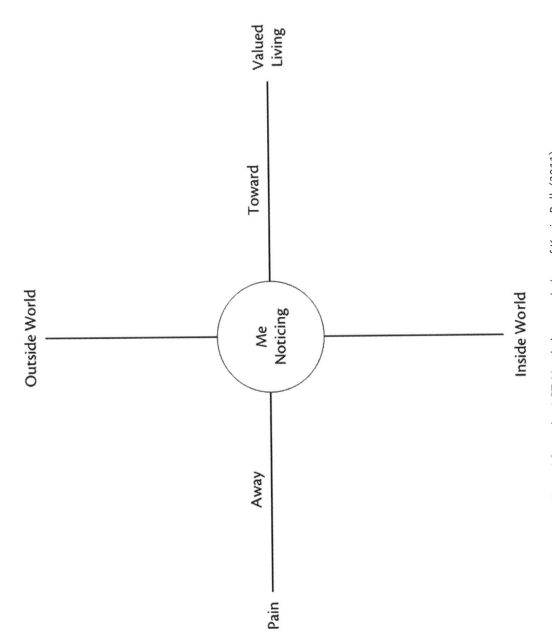

Valued
Living

Toward

Outside World

Me
Noticing

Inside World

Away

Pain

Adapted from the ACT Matrix by permission of Kevin Polk (2011)

TRAINING PHASE IV:

Building a Foundation for Valued Living

Building a foundation from which to engage valued living involves practicing and sharpening your Me Noticing skills. The process is similar to your weapons training during the academy. You probably first practiced the building blocks for shooting excellence, such as breathing, stance, grip, sight picture, sight alignment, trigger control, and follow through. With practice and over time, doing these things became more natural. Eventually, you did some target shooting and maybe some situational force-on-force shooting. However, you first focused your attention on practicing the fundamentals. The essence of the fundamentals remained the same despite the different shooting situations.

Good Breathing

Good breathing is the first building block for valued living. It gives you a sense of well-being and has important implications for your long-term health. Each breath you take contributes to balancing your body chemistry. Taking five or six breaths incorrectly alters it. Years of incorrectly overbreathing (hyperventilation) puts you at risk of developing health problems (Fried, 1999):

- Respiratory: asthma, tight chest, shortness of breath, sighing, or an irritable cough
- Cardiovascular: palpitations, tachycardia, or angina
- Neurological: dizziness, faintness, migraines, or numbness
- Gastrointestinal: dry throat, gas, belching, or abdominal discomfort
- Muscular: cramps, tremors, twitches, or muscle pain
- Behavioral health: tension, anxiety, depression, or phobias
- General health: fatigue, exhaustion, weakness, difficulty remembering or concentrating, sleep disturbances, or nightmares

Good breathing is also about the correct exchange of gases. You take oxygen into your body when you inhale. Oxygen enters your blood and circulates throughout your body, and your tissues and organs use it. Carbon dioxide is a by-product of your tissues and organs metabolizing oxygen. You get rid of this exhaust when you exhale. However, carbon dioxide has another important function. It's responsible for distributing oxygen to your tissues and organs and maintaining healthy body chemistry. Taking in the right amount of oxygen and getting rid of and using up the right amount of carbon dioxide yields better health.

Diaphragmatic breathing is good breathing (Fried, 1999). It uses the diaphragm muscle, which is a dome-shaped sheet of muscle separating your stomach cavity from your chest cavity. A respiratory cycle consists of an inhalation and exhalation. Your diaphragm and intercostal muscles contract when you inhale, which pulls the lower part of your lungs downward and moves your belly outward. Your muscles and lungs relax when you exhale, and they return to their resting positions, which moves your belly inward. Your diaphragm and intercostal muscles are the appropriate muscles to use when you inhale. When using your diaphragm and other muscles correctly to breathe, your belly rises and falls while your upper chest remains still.

The bottom line is that breathing well leads to being well. Breath training is an essential part of any effective life-skills training, counseling, or medical treatment program. Benefits of good breathing include deactivating the stress response, activating the calming response, generating pleasant feelings to live your values, increasing your situational awareness, strengthening your resiliency, improving sleep, lowering your heart rate, having less anger, and relieving pain.

Your overall goal in breath training is to breathe a little more slowly, deeply, smoothly, quietly, and evenly. Slowly inhale until you feel full. Slowly exhale until you feel empty. Breath training should feel comfortable, so don't force it.

Nasal breathing is healthier for you. It cleans, warms, and moisturizes the air you breathe. It helps you to regulate the speed of inhaling and exhaling. It promotes diaphragmatic breathing, whereas breathing through your mouth may lead to overbreathing. So breathe in through your nose and also out through your nose instead of your mouth.

Good breathing during training ranges between four and a half and seven breaths per minute (Lehrer, Vaschillo, & Vaschillo, 2000; Vaschillo, Lehrer, Rishe, & Konstantinov, 2002; Vaschillo, Vaschillo, & Lehrer, 2006). This translates to an average of around six breaths per minute—five seconds of inhaling and five seconds of exhaling. However, I want to clarify that you won't always be breathing between four and a half and seven breaths per minute. In fact, you shouldn't, because you must adjust your breathing rate to meet the metabolic needs of your daily activities. Some activities require you to speed up your breathing, such as chasing a suspect at work, or to slow down your breathing, such as reading at home. Your demand for oxygen changes throughout the day.

Think of your breath training as similar to strength training at a gym. If you lift weights for one hour a few times a week, then you'll increase your strength. There is no need to walk around holding dumbbells all day to maintain your gains. Similarly, if you practice breathing consistently for about five minutes or more several times daily and at a breath rate around six breaths per minute, then you'll exercise and strengthen your autonomic nervous system reflexes and maintain your gains.

Begin your breath training at a pace like your normal breathing rate. The average person breathes between twelve and fourteen breaths per minute. Then gradually bring your breathing pace down one or two steps at a time. More steps may be necessary if you're used to breathing very fast. On the way down, check whether you're breathing diaphragmatically and whether you feel OK, light-headed, dizzy, or sleepy (a little bit, moderately, or quite a bit) at each breath rate. Feeling light-headed, dizzy, or sleepy may be signs of overbreathing (hyperventilation, high-to-low ratio of oxygen to carbon dioxide) or underbreathing (hypoventilation, low-to-high ratio of oxygen to carbon dioxide). Your final breath-training rate should be at a pace at which you feel OK—somewhere around six breaths per minute.

Breathing below ten breaths per minute during training stimulates lower sympathetic and higher parasympathetic autonomic nervous system activity. The parasympathetic branch of your autonomic nervous system is responsible for slowing down your heart rate and promoting bodily recovery and rejuvenation following a stressor. It takes control after you try to move away from something painful.

In training, breathing at a rate below ten breaths per minute also counters a natural tendency toward autonomic nervous system imbalance: higher sympathetic activity in response to thinking painful thoughts and feeling difficult feelings in life. Prolonged trauma and stressor-related thoughts and feelings tend to produce a pattern of breathing faster and more shallowly (hyperventilation); generate irregular rhythms (incoherency) among your digestive system, autonomic nervous system, heart, and respiratory system (biological pacemakers); and sustain autonomic nervous system imbalance. All these things impact your overall health, well-being, and daily performance.

Breathing is a reliable, readily available method to achieve autonomic nervous system balance. The sympathetic and parasympathetic branches help you to act, react, and recover. At rest, your heart rate tends to go up (sympathetic stimulation) when you inhale and down (parasympathetic stimulation) when you exhale. Breath training increases the size and smoothness of these alternations in your heart rate, which are called heart rate variability. Consequently, you generate rhythm in your body and attain autonomic nervous system balance (Childre & Rozman, 2005).

Before you begin your breath training, be aware that diaphragmatic breathing may be strenuous. It may cause mild diaphragmatic cramping in some beginners and people in distress who hold their diaphragm in partial contraction. If you experience cramps and they get worse, persist, or cause discomfort, then you should discontinue the training.

One more thing is that diaphragmatic breath training may be inappropriate for people with particular physical conditions: muscle, tissue, and organ injuries; diabetes; kidney disease; low blood pressure; and related conditions. As with any exercise and training, consult a physician about your condition and whether diaphragmatic breath training is appropriate for you.

Exercise: Discovering How You Breathe Now

This exercise provides instructions for discovering how you breathe now.

Begin by sitting in a chair. Sit up so that your back is straight. Close your eyes, and start to notice your breathing…

Gently place your right hand over your belly button. Place your left hand on your chest. Use your hands to help you become aware of your breathing. Continue paying attention to your breathing for a few breathing cycles. Breathe in and breathe out…

What do you feel your hands doing? Your left hand on your chest should be still as you breathe in and out. Your right hand over your belly button should be moving out as you inhale and moving in as you exhale. If your right hand over your belly button moves more than the hand on your chest, then you're on the right track…

Continue to breathe, feeling your belly move under your right hand. Imagine a balloon in your belly filling with air as you breathe in. Then feel it deflating as you breathe out…

Now, relax your shoulders and arms, and return your hands to your lap with palms down and fingers naturally open…Gently open your eyes.

Exercise: Breathing Mechanics

This exercise focuses on practicing the mechanics of good breathing using your diaphragm muscle. It also activates feelings of appreciation and compassion that many people find pleasant.

Begin by finding a quiet place where you can sit in a chair and settle into a comfortable position…

Place your feet squarely on the ground. Sit up in the chair so that your back is straight but not rigid. Relax your shoulders and arms, and place your hands on your lap with palms down and fingers naturally open. Your head should feel level, looking forward. This posture helps you stay awake. There is nothing particularly difficult about doing this exercise. It just requires your attention.

Now you may close your eyes, or fix your eyes on a point in front of you.

Breathe in through your nose, feeling your belly expanding when you inhale, and out through your nose, feeling your belly contracting when you exhale…

As you inhale, feel the cool air flowing in through your nostrils, filling you up. With each inhale, imagine feeling appreciation…As you exhale, feel the warm air flowing out through your nostrils, emptying you out. With each exhale, imagine feeling compassion…

Continue practicing your breathing. As you exhale through your nose, feel the heaviness of your body. Its weight naturally falls downward, and its energy moves through your legs and feet and into the ground. Feel the sense of being grounded through your whole body...

Remember, breathe in through your nose, feeling your belly expanding, and exhale through your nose, feeling your belly contracting. Focus on breathing a little more slowly, deeply, smoothly, and quietly, relaxing more and more with each exhale. Practice for another two minutes or longer if you want. Gently open your eyes when you're ready.

Ideally, practice breathing at your breath-training rate a few times daily. There are phone apps available to help you practice by following a visual/audio breath pacer that you can set. Here is a sample training schedule that may work for you:

- When you wake up, practice for at least five to ten minutes.
- When you're at work, take two practice breaks (at least five to ten minutes each).
- Before you leave work, practice for at least five to ten minutes.
- Before you go to bed, practice for at least five to ten minutes.

During your breath training, you became aware of your body and belly movement. In trauma, it may feel like you are disconnected from your body, feeling numb, and no longer having a sense of yourself. However, you can rebuild this vital connection through body-awareness exercises, which you already began with your breath training.

The Mind-Body Connection

Trying to escape from painful trauma-related thoughts, feelings, and situations by numbing out to them with a drink, a painkiller, or something else is a survival strategy that disconnects you from your body. Any trapped animal, including you, will play possum. When the fight-or-flight options are unavailable in survival situations, the body slips into a default mode of freezing, feeling paralyzed, collapsing, and becoming immobile. Feeling dead and disconnected from your body lessens the pain of experiencing severe injury. It's a natural response, although your mind may tell you something different because of your police training.

Without the ability to actually act on a trauma memory or move away from it, you may get stuck and frozen in the trauma. To protect yourself, you learn to stop remembering and feeling. You become numb and lose connection with your body to avoid suffering pain. However, your body remembers. You can rebuild the connection between you and your body and begin feeling again. Here is a list of words to label different bodily feelings. You may also add other words.

Achy	Faint	Pounding
Blocked	Floating	Pressure
Breathless	Flowing	Queasy
Brittle	Fluid	Raw
Bubbly	Frantic	Shaky
Buzzy	Frozen	Spacey
Calm	Full	Streaming
Cold	Fuzzy	Strong
Cool	Heavy	Suffocating
Constricted	Hollow	Sweaty
Contracted	Hot	Tense
Dark	Icy	Thick
Deflated	Itchy	Throbbing
Dense	Jittery	Tight
Disconnected	Jumpy	Tingly
Dizzy	Knotted	Trembly
Dull	Light	Twitchy
Empty	Nervous	Warm
Energized	Numb	Wobbly
Expanded	Paralyzed	Wooden

Now that you have a vocabulary to name different bodily feelings, let's work on scanning the various parts of your body for different feelings.

Exercise: Scanning Bodily Feelings

Begin by lying down on your back, maybe on a cushy mat on the floor. Lie on your back with your legs uncrossed, your arms by your sides, your palms up, and your fingers naturally open. Allow your feet to fall naturally outward.

Either close your eyes or find a point on the ceiling to look at.

Start to become aware of your physical body...Begin to notice the different parts of your body, starting with your toes. Wiggle them a bit to help you focus there...Slowly scan from your toes to the bottom of your feet...Bring your attention around to the top of your feet, feeling that area of your body...Now, scan up to your calves. What do you feel there? Wrap around to the front of your lower legs, noticing your shins...

Scanning farther up, focus your attention on your knees, feeling the bend there...Move up to your thighs, feeling any sensations there...Now, go around to the back of your legs, getting a sense of your hamstrings. What do you feel there? Scan farther up to your hips and lower back, noticing any sensations in this area of your body...

Now, bring your attention around to the front of your body. Become aware of your belly...Scan up and become aware of your chest...Circle around and notice any sensations in your upper back and shoulder blades...Now, scan out from your shoulders to your upper arms. What do you notice in your biceps? Wrap around and notice your triceps...Now, scan down to your elbows, and notice any sensations there...Continue scanning down to your lower arms, and notice your forearms... Scan further to your wrists, and notice them. Notice your palms...and your knuckles...Scan out to the tips of your fingers...

Releasing your attention from the tips of your fingers, focus your attention now at the base of your neck. What do you notice there? Scan up your neck slowly, noticing any sensations along the way as you scan up to the back of your head...Scan around to the front of your head. Become aware of your chin...Begin to scan up, and notice the sensation of your lips... nose...cheeks...eyes...and forehead...Scan up now to your scalp. Become aware of any sensations there...

Releasing your attention from your scalp, notice your whole body lying on the floor. Become aware of those parts of your body making contact with the floor, and notice any sensations there...

Now, shift your attention to just breathing for the next thirty seconds. Gently open your eyes.

What sensations did you notice in your body? _____
_____
_____
_____

Where in your body did you notice them? _____
_____
_____

Were you more involved in following the exercise or more involved in wandering away to other things? Use the words "I'm noticing" in your response (for example, "I'm noticing I was more involved in following the exercise"). _____

Are you feeling better, about the same, or worse now? Use the words "I'm noticing" in your response (for example, "I'm noticing I'm feeling better"). _____

What did you learn from doing the exercise? _____
_____
_____

Did you have any difficulty sensing bodily feelings? _____

_____

_____

Exercise: Sensing Your Muscles and Skin

Besides scanning for bodily feelings, you can stimulate sensations in your body by rubbing your muscles and skin. The following exercise draws on ideas from the Finding Your Body Boundaries exercise (Levine, 2008).

Sit in a chair, and get into a comfortable position. You may also close your eyes, or keep them open if you prefer.

Using your right fingers, alternate between squeezing and rubbing your left forearm muscles. Squeeze and rub hard enough to feel the shape and density of the muscles…Notice all the sensations you're feeling there while squeezing, rubbing, and letting go…What do you feel? Maybe it's pressure, touch, or your blood flowing. Just notice whatever you're feeling…

Continue doing this exercise for the other muscle groups in your body: biceps, triceps, shoulders, trapezius, abs, quadriceps, hamstrings, and calves. Switch to using your left fingers for the right side of your body. Take enough time to feel the muscle groups.

Now, let's work on stimulating sensations in your skin. Using your right fingers, alternate between caressing and tapping the skin covering the palm of your left hand…Notice all the sensations you're feeling there…What do you feel? Maybe it's pressure or a chill. Just notice whatever you're feeling…

Continue caressing and tapping the skin covering the other parts of your body: forearms, upper arms, neck, scalp, face, and upper and lower legs. Switch to using your left fingers for the right side of your body. Take enough time to feel the skin covering your body.

Did you have any difficulty stimulating bodily sensations? _____
What feelings did you notice as you did the exercise? _____

_____

In what part of your body did you notice them? _____

_____

John's story. Initially, John had difficulty doing the exercise. He wasn't feeling very much. To jump-start his feeling again, we added taking a shower while doing the exercise. John also alternated the water temperature and the different patterns of water pressure. These things helped him wake up his mind-body connection.

Grounding

The last step in building a foundation from which to engage in valued living is grounding. Trauma reactions may feel as if they pull your legs out from under you, and you lose your ground. *Grounded* means being aware, present in your body, and connected to the ground beneath you. This experience gives you a sense that thoughts and feelings won't easily knock you off your feet and that you can move, take action, and get back into the stream of valued living.

In this next exercise, you'll explore the physiological and perceptual experience of being grounded. You may create your own recording of the exercise or download it at www.actforpolice.com.

Exercise: Body Grounding

Stand with your legs open, feet facing slightly outward and shoulder width apart from front to back and side to side (begin with your left foot forward and right foot back).

Hold your body erect, stretching your back muscles...Look around, becoming aware of your surroundings...Now focus your gaze at a point straight in front of you...

Feel your feet fully contacting the ground...and bring your attention to your breathing. Breathe in through your nose, feeling your belly expanding, and breathe out through your nose, feeling your belly contracting...As you exhale, feel the energy flow from your belly, through your legs, to your feet, and into the ground...Feel your whole body relax more and more, becoming heavier and heavier each time you exhale...Feel the sense of being grounded...Now, bend your knees and bounce a little bit. Notice the relaxation and flexibility in your legs and in the rest of your body...

Keeping your stance and moving from your belly, sway your body and arms slowly forward while you exhale through your nose (front knee bending and rear knee extending). Sway them slowly back as you inhale through your nose (front knee extending and rear knee bending). Move your arms as though you were rowing a boat...Do this again, but this time, raise your arms naturally forward to your shoulder height when swaying forward. Keep your hands open and fingers naturally spread. Lower them down to your sides when swaying back...

Keeping your stance, raise your arms naturally forward to your chest height. Keep your hands open and fingers naturally spread. Now, add stepping forward and imagining you're entering into a thought or feeling: your front foot advances first, and then your rear foot slides up, with your feet coming to rest in the same relative stance. Imagine touching the thought or feeling with your hand and feeling it pass by you as you continue to step forward to face the next thought or feeling. Alternate stepping forward with your right and left foot...

What did you notice as you did the exercise? _____

_____

_____

_____

In this physical exercise, loosening up your body, anchoring it, and staying flexible while moving prepare you to work with painful trauma-related thoughts and feelings when they show up in a situation. When you're able to move flexibly with your thoughts and feelings,

1. physical flexibility becomes psychological flexibility;
2. psychological flexibility shows up in a body that moves flexibly and holds itself confidently in strength and readiness; and
3. physically and psychologically you can face painful trauma-related thoughts and feelings squarely, be with them, and move with them.

The alternative would be that they knock you over, you run away from them, or you try to control them.

Another way to develop your sense of being grounded is by interacting with animals. Many animals, such as dogs, are naturally grounded—their weight sinks down naturally and continuously through their legs and into the ground. For example, place your hands on a dog's body while it's sitting or standing. Feel the dog's heaviness, how its body weight falls naturally, and how it makes contact with the ground. Feel the dog's heartbeat. Focus on its breath, feeling its belly moving outward when inhaling and moving inward when exhaling. Notice the dog's natural calmness when connected to the ground. You may also play with the dog by having it lie down on its back. You will notice how the dog naturally moves to turn over so that its weight is underside, and its paws connect to the ground.

Complementary movement practices to continue developing a felt sense of being grounded include aikido, yoga, tai chi, and qigong. These practices combine the benefits of breathing, moving, balancing, stretching, strengthening, and mindfulness into one practice.

So far, you've practiced exercises to activate and bring awareness to bodily feelings, regaining a sense of your body holding all your thoughts and feelings. You also practiced good breathing and grounding to help restore a sense of being present in your body and connected to the ground beneath you. Your new skills and resources will support your body as a stable platform from which to move and act, guided by your values. They'll also help you learn and practice new skills in the next phase of the training. What you'll do next is train up your ability to hold painful trauma-related thoughts and feelings inside you so that you can live your values.

Some Things to Practice

Take a break now from your training to complete the following action plan. Give yourself enough time—a few days or more—to complete it before you begin the next training session.

1. Practice the Breathing, Scanning Bodily Feelings, Sensing Your Muscles and Skin, and Grounding exercises.
2. Continue using the Crosshairs diagram to draw painful trauma-related life situations.

TRAINING PHASE V:
Staying with Your Pain

Ask yourself the following question: "What am I willing to experience and do in this situation to move toward what's important to me?" Being willing to stay with something painful that shows up in a situation opens you up to the other things the situation has to offer you.

Now, I understand that your mind may be telling you, *No, I don't want to do that. I want you to help me make it go away so it never comes back again.* I understand your mind wanting that. I understand its impulse to want to get rid of it. The research now, though, doesn't support that approach in the long run.

When I say "being willing," I'm not talking about being willing just for the sake of being willing. What if being willing were to get you moving in a direction toward what you want to be doing in life? What if you were to work on being willing for the purpose of getting you closer to your values?

In this training phase and the next one, you'll work on the process of being willing or the willingness to experience pain for the sake of living your values more fully without as much struggle with painful thoughts, feelings, and situations—and with renewed purpose and vitality (Hayes & Smith, 2005). Besides, how is being unwilling to experience that painful stuff working for you right now?

Training Up Your Willingness
Staying with painful trauma-related thoughts, feelings, and situations involves some new Me Noticing skills. Let's begin with noticing that pain associated with such thinking and feeling has a quality of uncertainty. Not knowing what will happen if you don't do something about your thoughts and feelings and the situation you're in right now triggers an urgency to act. The emergency comes in the form of an intense thought or feeling that lures you in; you bite it and get hooked (Chödrön, 2002). Feeling tense, tight, and rigid, not wanting to be there, and wanting to do something quickly to get off the hook: that's what being hooked feels like.

Exercise: Staying with Uncertainty
In this exercise, you'll practice staying with uncertainty, holding, and making room within you for painful thoughts and feelings without moving away as you habitually do. Staying still, you begin to loosen up and to soften your grip on the problem-solving approach to pain, and you realize you don't fall into a black hole.

Begin by finding a comfortable place where you can sit. Close your eyes, or fix your eyes on a point in front of you.

Start focusing on your breathing. Breathe in through your nose, feeling your belly expanding when you inhale, and breathe out through your nose, feeling your belly contracting when you exhale...

Continue paying attention to your body and your belly moving in and out during breathing while keeping your other body parts still...

As time passes, you may notice you feel an itch...You may also notice an urge to scratch or move...Allow yourself to have different thoughts and feelings without making any effort to change them. Welcome them in, and agree to meet them with friendliness, kindness, and compassion while staying still...

Continue remaining still as you notice different thoughts and feelings showing up. Remember, there is no need to respond to what your mind and body are telling you. Just observe what they're saying. Watch how what they say comes and goes like cars passing by outside your house, and bring your attention back to your breathing...

Now, in your mind, shift your attention to the image of the room...Gently open your eyes.

What thoughts came to your mind as you did the exercise? _____
_____
_____
_____

What feelings showed up as you did the exercise? _____
_____
_____

Did you find yourself scratching, moving, or doing something else when your mind and body told you to?_____
_____
_____

If so, what happened when you did it? Did you notice some relief? Did you feel better? Did those thoughts and feelings go away? Did you want to do it again? Did it make the situation worse? Did those thoughts and feelings come back again?_____
_____
_____
_____

_____

_____

_____

_____

If not, what happened? _____

_____

_____

_____

_____

_____

Were you more involved in following the exercise or more involved in wandering away to other things? Use the words "I'm noticing" in your response (for example, "I'm noticing I was more involved in following the exercise"). _____
_____

Are you feeling better, about the same, or worse now? Use the words "I'm noticing" in your response (for example, "I'm noticing I'm feeling better"). _____

What did you learn from doing the exercise? _____
_____

_____

_____

When you quiet yourself down and focus on (and stay present with) your breathing happening here and now, you'll notice that your mind repeatedly wanders away and that you always come back. After all, how would you know that your mind wandered away to thoughts and feelings if you didn't always return to something here and now, such as breathing in this exercise?

Staying with your breathing does not mean you're not thinking and feeling. Your mind is busy telling you all sorts of things all the time. You already have the ability to listen, pay attention, be present, and set aside what your mind tells you to do. For example, remember a time when you were talking with someone important to you, and your mind unexpectedly threw out a thought like _Slap the person_ or something like that? What did you do? Well, you probably didn't act on it, and you wondered where that thought had come from. In the huge network of thoughts in your mind, there was something about that moment linked to the words _Slap the person._

In watching your thoughts and feelings in a situation, pay attention openly, curiously, and flexibly (Harris, 2009). What I mean by "openly" is that you may not like or want the thoughts and feelings you're having, but you're not trying to avoid, get rid of, or escape from them. What I mean by "curiously" is that maybe your thoughts and feelings are helpful or maybe they're unhelpful in doing what's important to you in life. What I mean by "flexibly" is that you can zoom into and out of the thoughts and feelings you're having.

When painful thoughts and feelings show up, notice them, be patient with them, and get curious about them. In that moment of discomfort, know that there's a good chance they'll trigger your mind to think *Get away. Do what you've done before. It will work. It will make you feel better.* Does it? Will it this time? The best you can say is yes, briefly. However, somewhere you know it won't. Yet the urge to do the usual thing is still there in your mind and body. If you do it, then you'll feel better. In the long run, you're just strengthening habits that are keeping you stuck in your pain. Trying to move away from inescapable trauma-related thoughts and feelings cripples you from living your values.

The fact is, painful trauma-related thoughts and feelings come and go. They have a quality of impermanence.

Exercise: Watching Impermanence

The following exercise draws on ideas from the Soldiers in the Parade (Hayes et al., 2012) and Leaves on a Stream (Eifert & Forsyth, 2005) exercises. In the exercise, you'll practice watching your thoughts and feelings come and go and noticing when they pull you away from your experience. You'll become aware of their impermanence. So relax wholeheartedly into the fact that things change.

Begin by finding a comfortable position to sit in. Either close your eyes or fix your eyes on a spot in front of you.

Now, imagine sitting on a grassy bank next to a winding, gently flowing creek. As you look at the creek, you notice autumn leaves on the surface of the water. Keep looking at the leaves, watching them effortlessly make their way past you, down the creek, and out of your sight…

Eventually, you'll wander away to thinking thoughts and having feelings. When you notice yourself doing these things, put each thought or feeling—whether pleasurable or painful—on a leaf as it comes closer to you. Watch it drift away, go down the creek, and float out of your sight. Then return to just watching the creek and the leaves floating along…

As you're watching the creek, you may notice your mind drifting away again to thoughts and feelings and acting like a sense-making machine, trying to figure them out. Your mind may even try to fix what it's cranking out. That's just what minds do. As your mind is doing these things, you may notice that the creek seems to stop flowing, and the leaves are piling up in front of you. When that happens, you can say to yourself, *Ah, there's sense making* or *Ah, there's fixing.* Put them on leaves, and watch them drift away, go down the creek, and float out of your sight. Then return to just watching the creek and the leaves drifting along…

As you notice thoughts and feelings come into your mind, notice the temptation to buy into them. They lure you into the water, and unknowingly, you've hopped onto a leaf, and you're riding it down the creek. Everyone does at some point. When that happens, back up a few seconds, and try to catch what you were thinking and feeling just before getting lured into the water. Then put those thoughts and feelings on leaves. Watch them drift away, go down the creek, and float out of your sight until the next time you find yourself unwittingly on a leaf floating away...

As you're watching the creek, something else you may notice is that the creek never gets moving. Your mind starts cranking out thoughts like *It's not working* or *I'm not doing it right.* You may even get frustrated or upset. You can put those thoughts and feelings on leaves and send them sailing gently down the creek and out of your sight. Then return to just watching the creek and the leaves drifting along...

Releasing your attention now from the creek, shift your attention to just your breathing... Gently open your eyes.

What thoughts came to your mind as you did the exercise? _____
_____
_____
_____

What feelings showed up as you did the exercise? _____
_____
_____
_____

Could you picture the creek and autumn leaves? _____
Use the following lines to write about what happened during the exercise. Include any details about the leaves piling up when the creek stopped flowing or that it never got started or that you were lured into the water—and what you did next._____
_____
_____
_____
_____
_____
_____
_____
_____

Were you more involved in following the exercise or more involved in wandering away to other things? Use the words "I'm noticing" in your response (for example, "I'm noticing I was more involved in following the exercise"). _____
_____

Are you feeling better, about the same, or worse now? Use the words "I'm noticing" in your response (for example, "I'm noticing I'm feeling better"). _____

_____

What did you learn from doing the exercise? _____

_____

_____

_____

In this exercise, maybe you've noticed that the nature of thoughts and feelings is that they won't feel pleasant all the time. You'll experience unpleasant things in life despite your natural tendency to seek lasting thoughts and feelings that feel good. Trauma-related thoughts and feelings will come and go. Sometimes they hang around longer than other times, especially when they lure you in and you bite, get hooked, and do the habitual thing to move away. This just aggravates the pain and keeps you stuck in it.

> **John's story.** During the Watching Impermanence exercise, John got the sense of being stuck. The creek stopped flowing, and leaves were piling up in front of him. Just before it happened, John remembered thinking, *I'm not safe*. It showed up for only a couple of seconds. He put it on a leaf, and it was gone before he knew it.
>
> John began feeling fearful, anxious, and sweaty, and his heart started pounding a minute or so later. When I asked him where the thought *I'm not safe* had gone, he didn't know. He was just thinking and feeling. In other words, John's thought was thinking for him. He shifted from looking at his thoughts and feelings to thinking and feeling from them. At that point in the exercise, he got hooked. He had the sense of being stuck in the water with the leaves. John had no situational awareness. He couldn't see his thoughts and feelings for what they were—just thoughts and feelings—and where they were—only inside of him.
>
> Eventually, John got back to the point just before getting hooked. He put his thoughts and feelings on leaves and sent them sailing down the creek. John got stuck and unstuck a couple of times. I told him that I'd never met anyone who could let the creek flow all the time without having a sense of it stopping or being in it. Zen masters practice a lot, and they can't even do that. It's unrealistic to expect that.

Feeling stuck in painful trauma-related stuff is like being trapped waist-deep in the middle of a smelly, muddy swamp (Hayes et al., 1999, 2012). Your thoughts and feelings seem to bog you down. The key is walking through the swamp because it stands between you and the direction you want to travel in life. Getting muddy, feeling icky, smelling bad, and walking through the weeds are all in the service of living life guided by your values.

When you're willing just to have that stuck feeling as you live your values, it begins to change all by itself, because that's the nature of all feelings. Staying with it may feel like you're swinging backward to feeling worse. When you give it enough time, you'll eventually swing forward to feeling better.

Exercise: Swinging with Your Feelings

In this exercise inspired by Peter Levine's pendulation practice (2008), you'll work on moving into and out of your feelings in order to restore the natural swing of living life in which painful thoughts and feelings come and go. Breathing through your heart was inspired by Doc Childre and Deborah Rozman (2005).

Begin by sitting comfortably in a chair. Sit up so that your back is straight, and let your shoulders and arms relax with your hands on your lap. Gently push your feet into the floor, and get a sense of the ground beneath you…

Now, either close your eyes or fix them on a spot in front of you. Start to bring your awareness to your breathing, feeling your belly filling up as you breathe in and feeling your belly emptying as you breathe out…

Next, focus your attention on the area of your heart…Your heart is close to the center of your chest. Picture your breath flowing slowly and smoothly in and out through this area, radiating waves of well-being and pleasant feelings. Maybe it's a feeling of serenity or contentment. We'll call this area your heartfelt place…

Shift your attention now, and ask yourself, "How is my life stuck right now?" Stand back and just observe what your mind and body tell you…What thoughts do you see? What feelings do you see? As you watch from a distance and sense the space between you and what you're thinking and feeling, say to yourself, *Yes, that's there. I can see that there*…

Bring your attention now to within your body, and travel to your heartfelt place. When you reach this area of your heart, sense the ease, calm, and inner balance radiating from it…

Slowly and gently swing back to that place of feeling how your life is stuck now…Swing forward again to your heartfelt place…Swinging farther forward, picture doing something that matters deep in your heart—maybe having a loving relationship with someone important or doing whatever gives your life meaning…What do you feel in your body? Swing back now to your heartfelt place…Swing farther back to that place of feeling how your life is stuck now…Swing forward again to your heartfelt place…Again, swinging farther forward, picture doing something different that matters deep in your heart and gives your life meaning…What do you feel in your body? Now swing back to your heartfelt place…

Shifting your attention now in your mind, just focus on your breathing…Gently open your eyes.

What thoughts came to your mind as you did the exercise? _____

_____

_____

_____

What feelings showed up as you did the exercise? _____
_____
_____

Could you picture and feel your heartfelt place? _____
Use the following lines to write about what happened during the exercise. Include any details about your experience of swinging back and forth and of when you were centered. What thoughts came to your mind? What feelings showed up? What did you feel in your body? _____
_____
_____
_____
_____
_____
_____
_____
_____

Were you more involved in following the exercise or more involved in wandering away to other things? Use the words "I'm noticing" in your response (for example, "I'm noticing I was more involved in following the exercise"). _____

Are you feeling better, about the same, or worse now? Use the words "I'm noticing" in your response (for example, "I'm noticing I'm feeling better"). _____
_____

What did you learn from doing the exercise? _____
_____
_____
_____

So far in staying with your pain, you've been facing thoughts and feelings head-on like a ship pointing its bow (the front end) into the waves of a storm to plow through them in one piece and to stay on course while the water is choppy. It requires willingly accepting—you can't run from the waves—and acting to keep the bow headed into rough seas until the storm passes. Turning the bow away could roll the ship over and sink it.

In life, there may be times when things become really stormy. You might feel overwhelmed by trauma-related thoughts and feelings, such as frozen in fear, crushed by guilt, consumed with shame, or boiling in anger. It seems as if you can't talk about the experience, move, or do what's important to you. If it happens, then you may use the breathing technique that follows to help you stay present and grounded during an emotional storm so that you can steady the boat, steer through the storm, and engage in life, guided by your values.

Exercise: Heart Breathing during an Emotional Storm

Anytime and anywhere, you can practice this breathing technique inspired by Doc Childre and Deborah Rozman (2005). With regular practice, you're more likely to use it when an emotional storm shows up in your life.

Sit down somewhere, and close your eyes. Feel where your body contacts the ground by moving it a little...

Notice any painful thoughts and feelings you're having right now...and notice that they're in a body that you can control and move...so start to sense your breathing. Breathe in and out through your nose. Feel your belly expanding as you inhale for five seconds and contracting as you exhale for five seconds. Continue for thirty seconds.

With each exhale, feel the waves of energy flowing through your body and into the ground... Over the next thirty seconds, feel the sense of your whole body becoming more relaxed and heavy and being anchored to the ground.

Place your hand over your heart now, and feel the warmth and gentle touch of your hand... Imagine your breath flowing in and out through the area of your heart...For the next thirty seconds (or longer), picture your heart radiating a feeling of care toward someone or something important in your life...When you're ready, gently open your eyes.

What did you notice as you did the exercise? _____

_____

_____

Is it easier for you now to be present and engage someone or something important to you? _____
Do you have more control now over moving your body—arms, legs, and mouth? _____
What did you learn from doing the exercise? _____

_____

_____

As you get better at staying with your pain, you'll notice that sometimes thoughts and feelings go away. At times, you get a lot of distance from them, at other times, you feel better, and sometimes, all these things happen. However, these things won't always happen. You might get a little or no distance from your thoughts and feelings. You might feel worse or experience no difference in how you're feeling. Overall, the aim of the exercises is to get better at noticing. It's not to feel better. In the long run, though, people tend to feel better with practice and being less caught up in painful thinking and feeling.

With practice, you'll also get better at tracking the connections and interactions among thoughts, feelings, and situations. You'll notice thoughts and feelings for what they are (only thoughts and feelings) and where they are (only inside of you). The alternative would be feeling wobbly, trembly, and tingly, with your heart beginning to pound without your noticing the thoughts or situation triggering them. Then all of a sudden, you're thinking something bad is about to happen, and you have a panic attack. Thinking and feeling reinforce each other, generating more painful thoughts and feelings. Remembering to come back to the present situation keeps you from staying hooked.

In summary, here are five key dos and don'ts of staying with your pain:

Do	Don't
welcome and greet your thoughts and feelings with appreciation, kindness, and care.	try to avoid, get rid of, or escape from your thoughts, feelings, or situations.
pay attention to your thoughts and feelings with openness, curiosity, and flexibility.	think you already know what thoughts and feelings will show up in the situation.
practice to get better at noticing.	try to feel better.
give yourself a break.	beat yourself up for thinking and feeling.
give yourself space to choose how to respond to your thoughts and feelings.	react automatically to your thoughts and feelings.

What to Practice Next

Take a break now from your training to complete the following action plan. Give yourself enough time—a few days or more—to complete it before you begin the next training session.

1. Complete the Noticing Feelings exercise that follows.
2. Practice the Staying with Uncertainty, Watching Impermanence, and Swinging with Your Feelings exercises.
3. Continue using the Crosshairs diagram to draw painful trauma-related life situations.

Exercise: Noticing Feelings

In this exercise, you'll practice noticing different feelings. What will emerge in the exercise is the day-to-day traffic and chatter of unpleasant feelings that may hook you and trigger the problem-solving approach to pain. What you may also notice are pleasant feelings generated by living life guided by your values. So pick a few different times during the day to do the exercise.

Begin by pausing for a moment, taking a breath, and noticing any feelings you're having on the list that follows.

Say aloud what feelings you're having, using the following words before each feeling: "I'm noticing _____." Check it on the log by putting a slash mark.

You may also close your eyes and just name the feelings you're experiencing. You may add other feelings to the list, or use your own words to describe what you're feeling and add them.

Notice whether your mind tells you a story about why or how much you have the feeling. You don't have to listen to what your mind tells you. Just say aloud the feeling, and move on.

Day																	
Time																	
Frustration																	
Anger																	
Fear																	
Worry																	
Anxiety																	
Resentment																	
Distress																	
Hopelessness																	
Depression																	
Helplessness																	
Rejection																	
Sadness																	
Guilt																	
Worthlessness																	
Shame																	
Exhilaration																	
Passion																	
Joy																	
Happiness																	
Love																	
Enthusiasm																	
Caring																	
Appreciation																	
Compassion																	
Acceptance																	
Serenity																	
Contentment																	
Relief																	
Calmness																	

TRAINING PHASE VI:
Choosing a Life Direction

When you value things in life, thinking painful thoughts and feeling difficult feelings are a normal part of the human experience. In caring about or loving someone, there is the fear that the person will hurt you or get hurt. Working in policing and caring about protecting others gives rise to the fear that something bad will happen to you, your coworkers, or others. You see, pain is relative. It's something worth having because what you'll discover in it are things you care about.

To investigate this third quality of pain, let's begin by defining what values are and aren't. Remember, uncertainty and impermanence are the other qualities of pain that we covered in the previous training phase.

Things That Matter in Life

Who is important to you? Maybe it's your kids, spouse, family, friends, and coworkers. What areas of life and other things are important to you? Maybe it's work, family, spirituality, sports, and health. To move toward who and what are important to you in life, what do you want to keep on doing (gerunds), and how do you want to keep on doing it (adverbs)? These chosen actions are what we call values (Harris, 2009; Hayes et al., 1999, 2012; Polk et al., 2016). For example, maybe you want to be helping people competently at work. Where does this statement exist?

Values are statements in your head. They're thoughts that are available to you all the time (Harris, 2009). You can choose when, where, and how to act on them.

Values are your internal horsepower (or driving force) for living with purpose and vitality. Genuinely thinking about your values generates pleasant feelings such as joy, compassion, and caring. Having pleasant feelings can also energize thinking about your values.

Values are the directions you want to go in life. They're like compass headings keeping you on course toward valued living (Hayes et al., 1999, 2012). Do you ever reach your values? If you said no, then you are correct. Living your values is just like traveling west. You never actually reach it or get there as you do with results.

Results are what you want to get or have. Here are a few examples of how values and results are different. *Serving people expertly* is a value at work, whereas becoming a sergeant is a result. Serving people expertly is ongoing. You want to serve people this way despite what position you get or the job you have at work.

Interacting with family respectfully is a value (how you want to act), whereas being respected by family members is a result (what you want from others). *Loving my kids wholeheartedly* is a value in parenting, whereas being loved by my kids is a result. *Performing my job skillfully* is a value at work, whereas making a good arrest is a result. *Talking with people kindheartedly* is a value, whereas never being angry again at people is a dead person's result (Luoma et al., 2007). Only a dead person gets to do that—at least, that's what I think.

Values are chosen by you. You choose them because they are important to you and for no other reason. In the long run, your values may also be important to others.

Values aren't what others want for you or what you think *I have to do or I'm supposed to do*. Values aren't something to be right or wrong. There is no need to explain or defend them (Hayes et al., 1999, 2012). Values are like your favorite TV shows. There is no need to justify what you like to watch. However, you'll need to choose what to watch when you're with your family. In the same way, sometimes you need to prioritize which value to act on in a situation. For example, you value *relating with people caringly*. But if someone attacks you at work, then you defend yourself because you value *living life safely*, which takes priority.

Exercise: Constructing Values

What do you value in life? The following are some words for you to choose from and to construct values in areas of life that are important to you. You may also add other words. In the table that follows, I listed a few examples that John provided during our work together. Fill in the table with your values. You may also add other areas of life to the table.

What Do You Want to Keep on Doing?

Accepting	Connecting	Interacting	Nourishing	Sharing
Acting	Contributing	Leading	Nurturing	Speaking up
Advocating	Embracing	Learning	Performing	Supporting
Applying	Engaging	Listening	Planning	Talking
Behaving	Exercising	Living	Playing	Teaching
Being	Getting along	Loving	Providing	Upholding
Caring	Giving	Maintaining	Relating	Welcoming
Communicating	Helping	Making	Serving	Working

How Do You Want to Keep on Doing It?

Acceptingly	Creatively	Gently	Mindfully	Responsibly
Accurately	Curiously	Graciously	Modestly	Safely
Actively	Diligently	Gratefully	Openly	Skillfully
Admirably	Eagerly	Healthily	Passionately	Spiritually
Affectionately	Effectively	Helpfully	Patiently	Strongly
Appreciatively	Emotionally	Honestly	Patiently	Supportively
Attentively	Energetically	Honorably	Perceptively	Tenderly
Boldly	Enjoyably	Humbly	Positively	Thankfully
Capably	Enthusiastically	Industriously	Powerfully	Thoughtfully
Caringly	Ethically	Intelligently	Precisely	Truthfully
Compassionately	Expertly	Intentionally	Productively	Understandingly
Competently	Fairly	Intimately	Professionally	Usefully
Competitively	Faithfully	Kindheartedly	Proficiently	Vigorously
Conscientiously	Fearlessly	Kindly	Purposely	Warmly
Cooperatively	Forgivingly	Knowledgeably	Reflectively	Wholeheartedly
Courageously	Friendly	Lovingly	Reliably	Willingly
Courteously	Generously	Loyally	Respectfully	Wisely

Area of Life	What do you want to keep on doing?	How do you want to keep on doing it?
Family	*Interacting with my family*	*Enjoyably*
Friends		
Work	*Working with my coworkers*	*Effectively*
Education		
Health	*Living life*	*Actively*
	Living life	*Safely*
Recreation		
Spirituality		
Parenting		

Area of Life	What do you want to keep on doing?	How do you want to keep on doing it?
Community		
Intimate Relationships		

Now that you've constructed your values, where would you write them down in the Crosshairs diagram? If you said the bottom right, then you are correct. Remember, values are thoughts or verbal statements in your head. Look at John's Crosshairs diagram that follows, which now includes his values. At this point, fill in your Crosshairs diagram with your own values.

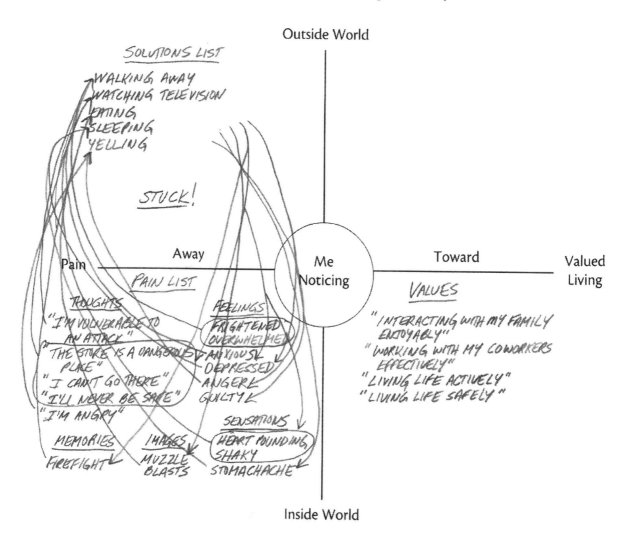

The Flip Side of Values

In the service of your values, you must be willing to do things that bring up pain so that you can change, heal, and grow. If you think about these things you value, then you'll usually find painful things on the flip side (Follette & Pistorello, 2007; Hayes et al., 1999, 2012). After all, if you didn't care about something, then you wouldn't have any pain around it. The following is a transcript of John and me doing an exercise to help him follow his values to find pain and follow pain to find his values.

Me: If you're willing, then I'd like us to do an exercise now to show how you can follow your values to find your pain and follow your pain to find your values.

John: OK.

Me: Let's start by your choosing a values statement you would like to work with.

John: Hmm...How about *working with my coworkers effectively*?

Me: OK. Here is an index card. What I would like you to do is write that statement down on one side of the card.

John: OK.

Me: Now flip the card over. On this side, I would like you to complete the following sentence and write down your answers in a bulleted list: In caring about *working with my coworkers effectively*, I fear that _____ .

John: What do you mean?

Me: For example, do you worry that something bad will happen?

John: Oh. OK. Hmm...I think *I'll make a mistake* or *I'll get someone hurt*.

Me: Those thoughts sound like more items on your pain list.

John: Yes.

Me: OK. Add them to your pain list. Now in thinking you'll make a mistake or get someone hurt, are there any painful feelings that come along with those thoughts?

John: Oh yeah! I feel anger, worry, fear, and some sadness.

Me: OK. Add them to the bulleted list. How about any feelings in your body?

John: Yes.

Me: What do you feel?

John: My stomach feels queasy, and my body is tense.

Me: OK. Add queasy and tense to the bulleted list.

John: Done.

Me: Excellent! Let's review what you have so far. On one side of the card, you're saying that you care about working with your coworkers effectively. On the other side of the card are the thoughts you'll make a mistake or get someone hurt and the feelings of anger, worry, fear, queasy, and tense.

John: Yes.

Me: OK. Let's say there is a way to get rid of all that painful stuff. The consequence would be that you no longer care about working with your coworkers effectively. So you would need to rip up that card and throw it in the garbage. After all, if you didn't care about working with your coworkers effectively, then you'd have no worry or fear about making a mistake or getting someone hurt, right?

John: Yeah. You're right.

Me: Now, do you remember when we first started our work together, I asked whether you would like to live life with more purpose and vitality, guided by your values, and you raised your hand?

John: Oh yeah.

Me: So you see, in valuing something in life, there's pain, and in that pain are your values. And the consequence of getting rid of the pain is giving up your values. You can't have one without the other. Now, do you want to hold on to your Values card, or rip it up and throw it in the garbage?

John: I want to keep it!

Me: OK. Let's now follow pain to find your values. Choose a thought on your pain list.

John: Hmm...How about *I'm vulnerable to an attack*?

Me: OK. Here's another index card. On one side of the card, what I would like you to do is create a bulleted list again. Write that thought down as an item.

John: Done.

Me: Now that you know the routine, what are some painful feelings that show up with that thought?

John: Fear, worry, nervousness, tense, pressure, and sometimes anger.

Me: OK. Write them down as items on the list. Now flip the card over. On this side, I would like you to complete the following sentence, and write down your answer: Thinking *I'm vulnerable to an attack* matters to me because I care about _____. Look at your values statements.

John: Ah! I get it now! It's *living life safely*.

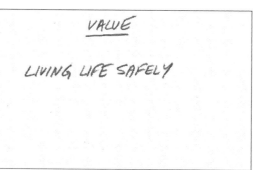

Me: Do you want to hold on to that card too?

John: Absolutely!

As you can see in my work with John, there's a lot of pain that comes along with valuing things, and in that pain are the very things you value. You may get rid of the pain—and with it goes your values. You may even try to move away from the pain by doing something on your solutions list—and with that goes the opportunity for living your values.

Take time now to create some Values cards as John and I did. Use the values statements you wrote down in the Constructing Values exercise, and use the items on your pain list. You may store your Values cards in a Rolodex if you want. You may also transfer each of them to a Crosshairs diagram.

To summarize, you can now use pain as an ally to trigger living life with more purpose and vitality, guided by your values. Here's how:

1. Take a breath, and pause for ten seconds.
2. Smile and thank your mind for the reminder that you care about something.
3. Think about that value.
4. Start doing something in the service of it.

Of course, having painful thoughts and feelings is also an opportunity to appreciate your values and all the pleasant stuff they bring you in life. Here are five key things to remember about what values are and aren't:

Values are	Values aren't
verbal statements in your head.	things outside of you.
chosen by you.	what others want for you.
how you want to act all the time.	what you want, get, or complete.
always available to act on right now.	in the future.
what's important to you.	something to explain or defend.

Did you have any difficulty constructing values in the previous exercises? Police officers, as do other people, sometimes find it hard to remember what's important to them when they've been living life on the left side of the Crosshairs. For example, in the Figuring Out Valued Living exercise, John forgot what he valued at work because he had been so busy dealing with the bullshit. Here are some ways to reconnect with your values:

- Ask yourself: "What do I disapprove of? What do I dislike in the actions of others? If I were in their shoes, then how would I act differently?" Remembering what you don't like, such as *I don't like people being disrespectful,* helps you remember what you value, such as *treating people respectfully.*
- Ask yourself: "Who do I look up to? Who inspires me? What personal strengths or qualities do they show that I admire?" Role models may be a source of behaviors you come to value.
- If, in the *ideal* world, you were living your life choosing what you want to keep on doing and how you want to keep on doing it, then what would you hear people say about you? How would they describe you? Ask two or three people important to you, such as your son, daughter, and spouse, "How would you describe me to a friend or stranger?"

Hooks, Willingness, and Getting Off the Line

Inescapable pain shows up when you're living life guided by your values. In phases IV and V of the training, you learned and practiced exercises involving staying, holding, and making space for painful trauma-related thoughts and feelings.

Being willing to stay with your pain is not giving up and just accepting it (Eifert & Forsyth, 2005). It doesn't mean that you want it to happen, you have to like it, you have to struggle through it, or you have to accept the situation that gave rise to it. It's not using a grin-and-bear-it strategy either. Staying with your pain takes courage—to hold on to something you can't control. Being willing, you can now use your time and energy to take action guided by your values, which you can control.

Being willing just to observe your mind yelling out all kinds of painful and scary things makes you "fear less." When you stop moving away as you habitually do from that stuff, the volume of painful thoughts and feelings goes down, their duration gets shorter, and fewer things provoke you. What you've been doing to get away from pain begins to fade into the background. It's as if you were playing baseball. I remember coaching my son's baseball team of ten- to twelve-year-olds and teaching them to field ground balls. I'd have them line up near third base to practice. Third base is a real hot spot for hits. The ball comes at you very fast with pull hitters. The goal is to field a ground ball hit to third base and to throw it to first base to get the hitter out. Doing this is in the service of valuing *playing baseball skillfully*.

Now, I tell the kids to keep their butts down, gloves in front of them, and eyes on the ball. I also say it may feel pretty scary at first because your mind tries to hook you on a story about how the ball will take a bad hop and hit you, and you'll get hurt. Besides, the kids are usually afraid of making a mistake or looking bad in front of their friends who are watching them.

When I begin hitting grounders to the kids, they usually do a couple of things to avoid the possibility of getting hurt. They turn their heads and look away or lift their heads, butts, and gloves off the ground and look away. It turns out that these things increase the chance of them getting hurt and making an error—and of their friends talking about or laughing at them.

However, when the kids are willing to keep their butts and gloves down and their eyes on the ball, they field the ball and throw it to first base to get the hitter out. The more they're willing to do it, the easier it gets, and the level of fear goes down. Sometimes the ball does take a bad hop, but the kids stay in front of it, knock it down, and still make the play to first base—all in the service of *playing baseball skillfully*. Even the pros worry about making an error, but the level of that stuff has gone down over their years of playing the game. Yet, sometimes, their minds still hook them on a story about missing the ball, especially after an error, and they end up having a bad game.

Even with your new Me Noticing skills and being willing, you are human. In life, painful thoughts and feelings lure us all in. You may exercise, meditate, fly-fish, see the values in your pain, and still want to punch someone in the mouth or say something mean. Trauma-related thoughts and feelings have a way of showing up and trying to provoke you, bully you around, and pull you out of the present situation and into the past or future. Before you know it, you're upset. You may end up doing things that only undermine your values, make you feel worse, or deny you what life has to offer you in the situation.

Here are some exercises to help you lean into painful trauma-related thoughts and feelings that tend to hook you so that you can change the way you relate to them when they show up in a situation.

Exercise: Stepping Back from Thinking

This exercise draws on ideas from the I'm Having the Thought That activity (Hayes et al., 1999, 2012).

Take out a blank piece of paper, and write down the thought *I'm angry*.

Tape the paper to a wall so that the thought is at eye level while you're standing. *I'm angry* is one of those all-time unfavorite thoughts about feelings that show up for many people, including police officers stuck in trauma.

Stand in front of the wall, take one step back, and look at the thought *I'm angry*.

Imagine being lured into *I'm angry* and getting hooked on it by giving it a posture, getting into the stance, giving it a voice, and saying the thought. For example, maybe you tighten your arms, make fists, and frown while yelling out as loud as you can, "I'm angry!" What's important is that you want to really lean into the thought *I'm angry* and be it.

Take another step back (two steps from the wall), and do it again, but this time you say the words "I'm noticing" in front of "I'm angry." So you would say, "I'm noticing I'm angry."

Take another step back (three steps from the wall), and do it again, but this time you say the words "I'm noticing I'm having the thought" in front of "I'm angry." So you would say, "I'm noticing I'm having the thought I'm angry."

Now do all three in order. Remember to step back each time, and lean into being the thought:

1. "I'm angry."
2. "I'm noticing I'm angry."
3. "I'm noticing I'm having the thought I'm angry."

What happened? Did you notice a sense of distance or separation from the thought *I'm angry*? Did you notice that *I'm angry* kind of lost its punch? If you didn't notice any distance from the thought, then that's OK too. You may do the exercise again using a different thought about a feeling on your pain list. Also, do it with other thoughts and feelings.

Let's try a different exercise to get unhooked when you hold tightly onto a painful thought you believe is true. The exercise is inspired by the Suitcase in the Sea metaphor (Harris, 2009).

Exercise: Letting Go of Your Grip

In this exercise, you'll work with an all-time unfavorite thought that some police officers hold tightly and believe to be true about a traumatic event. The thought goes something like this: *If only I had done something different*, then the outcome would have been different. Choose a thought similar to this one on your pain list. You may also decide to work with a different thought, as John did. He wanted to work with *I'm vulnerable*. Whichever you choose, pick one that you really believe is true.

What thought are you willing to work with today?_____

Now cut a piece of paper into two pieces about the size of your hand. Write down the thought on each piece of paper. Crumple them up, and hold on to one piece of paper in each hand. Close your hands, and squeeze them tightly. Keep on squeezing as hard as you can while you answer the questions that follow. You may write down your answers later.

When I hold this thought tightly, does it move me toward living my values? _____
_____

When I hold this thought tightly, does it help me do things in valued directions? _____
_____

When I hold this thought tightly, does it tie me up and prevent me from living my values? ____
_____
_____

Slowly open your hands, and allow the thoughts to fall out. As you do this, how do your hands feel? Do they feel kind of stiff and stuck at first? Do you notice the energy in your hands as your blood begins to flow again? Move your fingers around. Do you notice your hands loosening up and becoming more flexible to do things? Whether the thought is true or false, being willing to let go of your grip on it frees you up to use your energy to live the life you want to live. Don't forget to pick up your thought, and take it with you. After all, it's yours. You created it. However, you can hold it and carry it differently now, such as putting it in your pocket.

In this next exercise, you'll build on the grounding exercise that you practiced in phase IV of the training. You'll work on the fact that sometimes painful thoughts and feelings are just there, hanging around as if they were a body standing still. Other times, they may appear to your mind as growing and rapidly approaching threats of harm as if they were "a body in motion" coming at you (Riskind, 1997, p. 688). Being able to move flexibly with your thoughts and feelings frees you up to live your values.

Exercise: Verbal Aikido

On a piece of paper, write down something that you wanted to do in the service of one of your values, but painful trauma-related thoughts or images showed up and distracted you from doing it. In John's story, the activity was eating dinner with his family at their favorite restaurant in the service of John caring about *interacting with my family enjoyably*.

Place a chair on one side of the room, and put the piece of paper on it.

Look at your pain list. Remember a time when you wanted to do what you wrote down on the piece of paper, but a painful trauma-related thought or image showed up. What is the thought or image? _____

That's what you'll work with in this exercise.

Rate on a scale from 0 (not at all distressed) to 100 (completely distressed) how much distress you're feeling right now. _____

Stand back from the chair about five to ten steps.

Get into the stance that you practiced in the Body Grounding exercise in training phase IV. Stand with your legs open, feet facing slightly outward and shoulder width apart from front to back and side to side (begin with your left foot forward and right foot back). Hold your body erect, stretching your back muscles. Look forward at what you've wanted to do (written down on the piece of paper). Feel your feet fully contacting the ground. Bend your knees, and bounce a little bit. Notice the relaxation and flexibility in your legs and in the rest of your body.

Give yourself verbal cue one: "Begin thinking about doing the activity." Continue for five seconds.

Give yourself verbal cue two: "Pain shows up; notice it." Imagine the painful thought or image as though it were a body standing still, about two steps in front of you, with its right arm extending and making a fist at you. It stands between you and the activity you've wanted to do. Now, bring your focus to the arm, and immerse yourself in imagining that the arm is the painful thought or image. Continue for five seconds.

Give yourself verbal cue three: "Enter; be with it." Keeping your stance, move into the painful thought or image (the arm) by advancing your front foot first, and then your rear foot slides up, with your feet and body coming to rest in the same relative stance but angled toward and along the outside of the thought or image. Continue for five seconds.

Give yourself verbal cue four: "Make contact with it; have compassion for it." Gently raise your right arm naturally forward to your chest height. Keep your hand open and fingers naturally spread. Using your right hand, gently touch the painful thought or image. Don't grab or hold on to it. Continue for five seconds.

Give yourself verbal cue five: "Let it go; achieve your goal." Put your arm down, walk toward the chair, pick up the piece of paper, close your eyes, and imagine doing the activity. Just immerse yourself in imagining doing it. Continue for thirty seconds.

Repeat this sequence ten times: five times giving yourself all the verbal cues and five times giving yourself only verbal cues one and two.

Rate your distress at the end of the exercise. _____

Rate the highest level of distress that you felt during the exercise. _____

What did you notice as you did the exercise? _____

_____

_____

Were you more involved in following the exercise or more involved in wandering away to other things? Use the words "I'm noticing" in your response (for example, "I'm noticing I was more involved in following the exercise"). _____

Are you feeling better, about the same, or worse now? Use the words "I'm noticing" in your response (for example, "I'm noticing I'm feeling better"). _____

As you practice working with your thoughts or images in this physical exercise, you can also imagine them showing up with more intensity, such as a body moving toward you or punching at you. You can work with other people and have them perform the movements. To increase the intensity even more, you may have them add sounds to a punch, such as a *kiai* used in Japanese martial arts. It's a short yell or shout when performing an attacking move.

You don't always need to step forward with the left foot either. Step forward with your right foot instead. Have the attacker aim the strike at your head, chest, or stomach. Have multiple attackers representing different thoughts or images come at you. You can also construct different goals to accomplish and work with feelings if you want. To continue this type of practice, you may consider training in aikido. It's a Japanese martial art that literally means "the way to harmonize with energy."

Given your human ability to mentally represent things in your head, the overarching goal of this exercise was to construct how your trauma-related thoughts or images may show up and feel as though they are moving toward you at a frightening speed to cause you harm even though they can't hurt you. Instead of painful thoughts and feelings hooking you and triggering you to use needless defenses, such as the ones on your solutions list, you can practice willingness. And you can treat your painful thoughts and feelings with kindness and understanding, which gives you space to move and use your energy to live life guided by your values as you did in this exercise.

These next two exercises are also highly effective. They involve playing around with your painful thoughts and feelings (Harris, 2009; Hayes et al., 1999, 2012):

- Say your thoughts or feelings in a voice of someone who makes you laugh, such as your favorite comedian, cartoon character, or sportscaster, or say them using a funny accent.
- Sing your thoughts or feelings to your favorite song or music style, such as jazz, disco, or rock and roll, and dance to them.

You may also think up other kinds of fun things to do on your own. Playing around with your thoughts and feelings is not disrespecting them or your trauma. What you're doing is learning new ways of being with them so that you can live more fully, feeling greater purpose in your life.

What's more is that being playful helps you lean into painful thoughts and feelings and hold them lightly, allowing you to unhook from them, step back, and create space to observe them for what they are and where they are, instead of what your mind says they are.

As the master fly-fisher knows the type of flies to tie for fly-fishing, your mind knows just the type of thoughts and feelings to cast out for you to bite and to hook you. The harder you try to get off the hook by doing your away moves, the deeper your mind sets the hook. However, when you stop struggling and fighting to get off the hook, and you notice the values in your pain, you'll also notice that these types of hooks have no barbs. You can open your mouth, allow the hook to float away, and keep swimming in a direction you want to go in life until the next time your mind throws out some bait for you to bite.

Before we end with some practice stuff to do between training sessions, be sure to keep your updated Crosshairs diagram, Constructing Values worksheet, and Values cards for a training exercise on the horizon.

Getting Some Practice In

Take a break now from your training to complete the following action plan. Give yourself enough time—a few days or more—to complete it before you begin the next training session.

1. Notice any painful trauma-related thoughts and feelings that show up in a situation, whether they lure you in, whether you bite and get hooked, and what you do next. Use the Crosshairs diagram to draw any situation in which you got hooked—and what you might have done to get off the line.
2. Continue the Noticing Feelings exercise.

TRAINING PHASE VII:
Taking Committed Action

Let's begin this last phase of your training by talking about inertia. Inertia is a property of matter. Matter continues in its existing state of rest or motion unless some force changes its state. In other words, an object at rest tends to stay at rest, and an object in motion tends to remain in motion. For example, you step onto a train and sit down. The train begins to move. Before you know it, the train is traveling down the track, tooting its horn happily, and taking you where you want to go. The faster the train goes, the more momentum it generates to stay in motion. And it takes a lot of friction to slow down the train and stop it.

At rest, the train tends to stay at rest. Rust begins to form and corrode the train's wheels, engine, and body. It builds up after a while and makes it harder for the train to get moving again. A train sitting for two days is more difficult to get moving than a train sitting for one day. A train sitting for a month is even more difficult to get moving. How long have you been sitting, no longer doing what you used to do?

Moving builds momentum. Doing things creates momentum. In this phase of the training, you'll work on getting your ass moving and keeping it moving through committed action. Once you get moving, momentum takes over and propels you into living your values.

What Is Committed Action?

Committed action is a process of creating a life guided by your values (Hayes et al., 1999, 2012). Since you began your training, you've been taking committed action, such as reading this book, doing a breathing exercise, tracking feelings, and practicing. All these activities are guided by and moving you in directions you want to travel in life—your values, such as *living healthily*.

Taking committed action involves four basic steps (Harris, 2009): choose an area of life for action, choose a value to guide your action, develop a values-based goal, and track your action. Before we begin, you'll need a new Crosshairs diagram to fill in during this part of your training. Also, take out the Crosshairs diagram, Figuring Out Valued Living worksheet, Constructing Values worksheet, and the Values cards you completed already. Have them ready. You'll use them in the committed action steps that follow to tie together your training.

Step One: Choose an Area of Life for Action

This exercise draws on ideas from the Classroom Professor metaphor by Jill Stoddard (Stoddard & Afari, 2014). Imagine you're attending a college commencement. The guest speaker sets up an eight-foot table, drapes a cloth over it, places several boxes under the table, and sets a large beaker on the table. He looks at the audience, reaches under the table, pulls out a large box, and opens it up. He raises the box, which contains big rocks, and begins to dump some of them into the beaker. He shakes the beaker, dumps more big rocks into it, shakes the beaker again, and finishes dumping the rest of the big rocks so that the beaker is filled to the top. He looks out at the audience and asks, "Is the beaker full?" The audience says yes. What did you say?_____

The speaker reaches under the table again, pulls out another large box, and opens it up. He raises the box, which contains small rocks, and begins to dump some of them into the beaker. He shakes the beaker so that the small rocks fill the spaces between the big rocks. He dumps more small rocks into the beaker, shakes it again, and finishes dumping the rest of the small rocks so that the beaker is filled to the top with big rocks and small rocks. He looks out at the audience and asks, "Is the beaker full?" The audience says yes. What did you say? _____

The speaker reaches under the table again, pulls out another large box, and opens it up. He raises the box, which contains sand, and begins to dump some of it into the beaker. He shakes the beaker so that the sand fills the spaces between the big rocks and small rocks. He dumps more sand, shakes the beaker again, and finishes dumping the rest of the sand so that the beaker is filled to the top with big rocks, small rocks, and sand. He looks out at the audience and asks, "Is the beaker full?" The audience says yes. What did you say? _____

Now you're getting a little suspicious of this guy. He reaches under the table again, pulls out another large box, places it on the table, opens it up, and pulls out a jug of water. He raises the jug and pours some of the water into the beaker. He shakes the beaker so that the water flows between the big rocks and small rocks and through the sand. He pours more water, shakes the beaker again, and finishes pouring the rest of the water so that the beaker is filled to the top with big rocks, small rocks, sand, and water. He looks out at the audience and asks, "Is the beaker full?" Thinking this guy is not going to fool us again, the audience says no. What did you say?

The speaker finally replies and says, "Yes, it's full. What do you want to fill your beaker with? Put the big stuff in first. You can always add the small stuff later."

What's the big stuff that you want to work on first? To help you choose an area of life for action, follow John and me as we work together on this task.

Me:	Before we begin working on creating committed actions, let's look back at your responses to the Figuring Out Valued Living and Constructing Values exercises. Take out those worksheets and your filled-in Crosshairs diagram.
John:	OK.
Me:	Now, on the table, order them from left to right, beginning with the Crosshairs diagram, Figuring Out Valued Living worksheet, and then the Constructing Values worksheet. Look at the Figuring Out Valued Living worksheet and your answers in the "A" boxes. Which area (or areas) of life have the highest positive answer?
John:	Family and Health. They're both eights.
Me:	OK. Now remember, these are the areas of life that you noticed are the most shut down for you. In other words, you aren't doing very much, despite how important they are to you. Is that right?
John:	Yes.
Me:	And are they still high-priority areas where you want to start doing more things?
John:	Yes.
Me:	There's one more thing I'd like to confirm with you. Look at your Crosshairs diagram and your problem-solving approach to pain. Are these the things you've been doing that are knocking you off course from the things you've wanted to do in the areas of Family and Health?
John:	Yes.
Me:	OK. So which area of life do you want to work on first?
John:	Health.
Me:	OK. Look at the things you value in this high-priority area.
John:	I'm good to go.
Me:	Great.

Just as John chose his high-priority areas of life for action, choose one of yours now. Remember, high-priority areas of life are the ones most affected by your problem-solving approach to pain.

Step Two: Choose a Value to Guide Your Action

Look at your Constructing Values worksheet. In your high-priority area of life for action, select a value that you want to act on in the next twenty-four hours. Write down the value in your new Crosshairs diagram.

Step Three: Develop a Values-Based Goal

Now remember the Constructing Values exercise. We talked about how values are like compass headings that give you direction and keep you on course toward valued living, but you never really get there or reach them. Goals, on the other hand, are values-based actions that you do. They move you along the way. They're like the islands that you stop at and do things.

Goals bring your values to life. They involve what you do with your body that other people would notice if they were present. For example, maybe it's playing basketball, running in the park, talking with your son, and so on. Where would you write these things down in the Crosshairs diagram? If you said the top right, then you are correct. Here is an example of John developing a goal guided by his value *living life actively.*

John's story. John used to jog about fifteen miles per week. But since the trauma, he's been too busy trying to manage painful thoughts and feelings that show up. John has stopped jogging for more than six months. We talked about not biting off more than he could chew and building back up to where he was before. He agreed that it was unrealistic to start doing his old jogging routine right away. Doing that would probably cause him more pain, such as sore muscles, joint aches, or even an injury. So instead, John took little steps toward *living life actively.* A practical first step for him was walking for thirty minutes the next day and at least three times over the next week.

When it comes to developing goals, John developed a **S**pecific, **M**eaningful, **A**ction-oriented, **R**ealistic, and **T**ime-framed goal. We'll call it a SMART goal.

Specific
What exactly do you want to do physically in the world outside of you? For example, John initially scheduled a vague and nonspecific goal: "I want to exercise more." Although someone could see John exercising, the goal wasn't specific enough. What did John mean by exercise? What specifically did he want to do with his arms and legs? John identified walking as a new specific action to complete.

Meaningful
Confirm how well aligned what you want to do is with your value (Dahl, Wilson, Luciano, & Hayes, 2005). Ask yourself whether any of the following are guiding your action in the present situation: "Am I trying to move away from something painful? Am I trying to do what others want me to do? Am I trying to do what I think I'm supposed to do?"

Let's do an exercise now to help you get a sense of whether your values are genuinely driving your goals.

Exercise: Living Your Values versus Living Someone Else's
Think about something very specific that you've wanted to do in a high-priority area of life. The activity whips up lots of positive feelings. Maybe it's having dinner with someone important to you. In John's story, it was jogging on a treadmill. Once you have the activity in your mind, close your eyes.

Imagine you're standing about ten feet away from the activity and watching yourself doing it. Notice what you're thinking and feeling. Maybe you're feeling excitement and thinking *I can't wait to do it...*

Start walking slowly toward the activity. Feel your excitement and energy building as you walk toward what you've wanted to do for a while now. When you reach the edge of the activity, stop. Feel the excitement and energy in your body trying to push you into doing it, but wait and watch...

Now, jump into the activity, and do it. Completely immerse yourself in doing the activity...Feel all the pleasant feelings it's generating inside you. Maybe it's exhilaration, appreciation, joy, or happiness...Where do you feel it in your body?

Keep doing the activity because it's what you want to do. It's what brings you joy...As you're doing the very thing that you've wanted to do for a while now, you see a person in front of you. The person starts walking toward you. As the person gets closer to you, the person points a finger at you, waves it up and down, and commands, "You keep doing it! That's right, you keep doing it until I tell you to stop! Don't you stop! I'll tell what to do!" The person just keeps waving that finger at you, bullying you around, and commanding you to keep doing it...

Gently open your eyes now. What did you notice as you did the exercise? _____

_____

_____

_____

Some police officers say things such as "It felt great doing it." But when that person came along, "I got distracted. He pissed me off. I argued with him. I told him to fuck off. I hated doing it. It sucked." Doing what others want you to do or doing what you think you're supposed to do is as if you're listening to that finger-pointing person.

Other police officers say things such as "I saw the person. I felt a little annoyed at first but just kept doing what I was doing. I actually forgot the person was even there." That's committed action—being willing to experience pain and, in its presence, taking action consistent with your values.

Let's do another activity that involves the finger-pointing person. Imagine you set your alarm for 5:15 a.m. to wake up and exercise before work. The alarm goes off and wakes you up.

What are you thinking?_____

_____

_____

_____

What are you feeling? _____

_____

_____

What do you do now? _____

_____

_____

_____

Here's what happened in one of my exercise stories. My mind, right away, tells me that *I gotta do it*. It then says, *But I'm tired*. So I hit the snooze button to sleep seven more minutes. As I'm lying in bed, my mind is trying to convince me to go back to sleep. It tells me, *I can go jogging after work*. I begin arguing with my mind about whether to get up. Finally, I let out a long sigh of frustration, roll out of bed, dress, and go jogging. As I'm jogging, I start to feel better. I'm thinking about *living healthily*. And my mind tells me to *run more today* because I'm feeling really good now.

In my exercise situation, a few things are going on. After the alarm goes off, my mind tells me *I gotta do it*. For me, that's the finger-pointing guy. He wants to bully me around and tell me what to do. So my mind pulls me in the opposite direction and gives me reasons not to do it, which causes me more pain. Despite the pain, and certainly despite being unmotivated, I just do it. Once I start running, momentum takes over. I'm now feeling good, which gets me thinking about my value—*living healthily*—and wanting to run more. You see, motivation may be sufficient to get moving, but it's unnecessary. Getting moving is both necessary and sufficient for change.

Something else that may happen to me is thinking all the time that *I gotta do it*. It contaminates my value—*living healthily*. I end up no longer seeing the value in jogging. I'm just doing it because I think *I gotta do it* to avoid the possibility of painful results, such as the thought that *I'll get sick*.

It's also possible that my value—*living healthily*—turns into a rule that I must follow. Jogging now becomes a dreaded job *I gotta do*. So be aware of how your values can easily turn into rules that spin up the finger-pointing person in you.

To check on whether your values are driving your actions, pause several times a day, and ask yourself the following question: "Is what I'm doing right now in this situation moving me in a direction I want to go in life?" You won't need to answer it with words. You'll know just by what you're doing and how you're feeling. Living your values tends to generate pleasant feelings that let you know you're hitting the target.

Action Oriented

Be sure that what you want to do involves moving your body so that other people would notice if they were present. Simply put, what will you do with your arms, legs, or mouth? Maybe it's watching a movie with your family, writing a report, talking with a friend, and so forth.

A goal is not what you'll never do again, what you want to stop doing, or what you're trying to avoid. These are a "dead person's goals" (Luoma et al., 2007, p. 161). A dead person will never drink alcohol again, never yell again, and never argue again with someone important. Remember, you can't do what you want by never doing something else.

Another thing to look out for is doing something in the service of never doing something else. It's a signpost that you're living on the left side of the Crosshairs diagram. For example, you're sitting and watching television so that you never fall off the wagon again. Doing this requires time. You need to work at it. When you're doing it, time may seem to drag by. Getting moving in a valued direction feels like it takes forever. However, time flies when you're doing what you want your life to be about, and you're having fun.

When a "never" shows up, you can change it into a values-based goal by asking yourself, "What would I like to do instead of _____ in the service of my value _____?" For example, John came up with a goal of "I'll never argue with my wife again." I asked him whether there was something that he would like to do with his wife instead. He said, "Take her out to dinner." I asked him which value this act served. He said, "Interacting lovingly with my wife."

Realistic

Be practical about whether you can achieve what you want to do. Do you have the resources? Think about things such as your health condition. A back or knee injury, for example, may limit what you can do, such as running as often as you used to do. What can you do instead? For me, given my injuries, power walking when my back is hurting has become a workable alternative to jogging in the service of *living healthily*.

In John's story, jogging fifteen miles per week was an unrealistic goal to start with. He took small steps instead, set himself up for success, and didn't bite off more than he could chew:

1. Power walk thirty minutes three times for a week.
2. Power walk ten minutes and jog five minutes (twice) four times for a week.
3. Power walk five minutes and jog ten minutes (twice) four times for a week.
4. Jog thirty minutes five times per week.

When setting goals, notice that your mind may want to pull you toward when you were operating at your best. As John did with jogging, you may need to *take smaller steps* to achieve your goals. Here's another example of taking smaller steps to move you a little farther in a valued direction. Becoming a sergeant requires having an undergraduate degree. If you don't have one, then you'll want to begin searching the web for potential colleges to attend and earn one, which also requires multiple steps. Little by little, you'll get there.

What about the available time you have to complete a goal? In a work day, you may sleep seven hours, work eight hours, drive to and from work one hour, make and eat dinner one hour, and exercise one hour (totaling eighteen hours). This leaves you six hours to do other things, so you'll need to keep in mind any competing values. Given the time you have available, schedule a realistic goal to achieve.

Money may be something you need to consider. How about your skill set? Ask yourself whether you actually have the skills to do what it takes to achieve your goal. In some cases, you need to develop new skills before you can complete a goal. Suppose you want to parachute, and you've never done it before. There are a few things that you need to learn, such as packing your rig, before jumping out of a plane.

Lastly, be practical about falling short of accomplishing a goal. Everyone does. It's bound to happen, especially the first time you plan to do something different. It's unrealistic to think you'll always accomplish a goal whenever you say you will. Obstacles may come up, get in the way, and knock you off course. Maybe you're sick, someone isn't home when you call, or your friend has other plans. Maybe you get hurt or have financial responsibilities or perhaps a painful thought or feeling shows up and hooks you.

Time Framed

When setting any goal, be as accurate as possible about when you'll do it. As soon as you complete it, mission accomplished. You can check it off.

You can choose to do a values-based goal right now or aim to do one in a few hours, days, weeks, months, or years from now. An *immediate goal* is something you do within the next twenty-four hours. A *short-term goal* is something you do in a couple of days or a week. A *medium-term goal* is something you do in a couple of weeks or a month. Taking these small steps gets you moving. They're just as important as the big steps you take in completing long-term goals. A *long-term goal* is something you do a few months or years away. The following is a list of goals that John created:

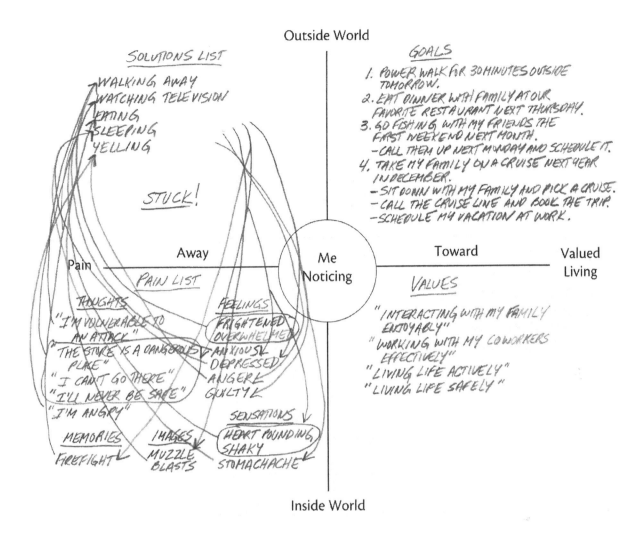

Outside World

SOLUTIONS LIST
WALKING AWAY
WATCHING TELEVISION
EATING
SLEEPING
YELLING

STUCK!

GOALS
1. POWER WALK FOR 30 MINUTES OUTSIDE TOMORROW.
2. EAT DINNER WITH FAMILY AT OUR FAVORITE RESTAURANT NEXT THURSDAY.
3. GO FISHING WITH MY FRIENDS THE FIRST WEEKEND NEXT MONTH.
   - CALL THEM UP NEXT MONDAY AND SCHEDULE IT.
4. TAKE MY FAMILY ON A CRUISE NEXT YEAR IN DECEMBER.
   - SIT DOWN WITH MY FAMILY AND PICK A CRUISE.
   - CALL THE CRUISE LINE AND BOOK THE TRIP.
   - SCHEDULE MY VACATION AT WORK.

Pain   Away   Me Noticing   Toward   Valued Living

PAIN LIST

THOUGHTS
"I'M VULNERABLE TO AN ATTACK"
"THE STORE IS A DANGEROUS PLACE"
"I CAN'T GO THERE"
"I'LL NEVER BE SAFE"
"I'M ANGRY"

FEELINGS
FRIGHTENED
OVERWHELMED
ANXIOUS
DEPRESSED
ANGER
GUILTY

VALUES
"INTERACTING WITH MY FAMILY ENJOYABLY"
"WORKING WITH MY COWORKERS EFFECTIVELY"
"LIVING LIFE ACTIVELY"
"LIVING LIFE SAFELY"

MEMORIES   IMAGES
FIREFIGHT   MUZZLE BLASTS

SENSATIONS
HEART POUNDING
SHAKY
STOMACHACHE

Inside World

You're now ready to develop a SMART goal. Here is a simple checklist to summarize what we've talked about:

- **S**pecific: What do I want to do?
- **M**eaningful: Is it aligned with my value?
- **A**ction oriented: Does it involve moving my arms, legs, or mouth?
- **R**ealistic: Can I achieve it? Does it require steps?
- **T**ime framed: Specifically, when am I going to do it?

Now look at the area of life and the value for action that you wrote down in the Crosshairs diagram. In the top right section, write down a corresponding SMART goal that you're 100 percent willing to commit to doing within the next twenty-four hours. Include any action steps necessary to complete the goal.

Next, list in the Crosshairs diagram any items on your pain and solutions lists that you think may show up in, get in the way of, or knock you off course from accomplishing your goal, such as what's happened in the past when you've tried to change your behavior and to do something different. To help you with this, look at the Crosshairs diagram and the Values cards you've completed already.

By now, you know that your mind tends to tell you what to think, how to feel, and what to do. When you create a road map that includes potential obstacles in the way of valued living, you're preloading a mental playbook to help you turn an "oh shit" moment into a valued living one.

Step Four: Track Your Actions

Are you paying attention to what you're doing at all levels? What are you doing in the outside world? What are you doing in the inside world? What are you doing to move away from pain? What are you doing to move toward valued living? Keep track of your actions in different situations—how and whether they help you accomplish your stated values-based goals—and notice their results. What did you think and feel? What did you do next? Were you successful? What did you get? Record these things by drawing them in the Crosshairs diagram.

John's story. Drawn next is the situation in which John completed his immediate goal, to power walk for thirty minutes the next day in the service of *living life actively* (value). Initially, John wrote down items on his pain and solutions lists that he typically did instead of exercising. When the next day came, he dressed up to exercise. Just before going outside to start walking, the thoughts *I can't go outside; it's too risky* showed up in his head. John felt and a little shaky. He took a breath, paused, and thought, *Ah, there's the value—I care about living life safely. This isn't work.* John smiled and laughed a little. He felt happiness and thought about *living life actively.* Then, he walked outside and power walked for thirty minutes around his neighborhood. After walking, John felt exhilaration and joy. His body felt energized and warm, and he could feel his blood flowing again. John thought, *I feel great.*

The Situation: *THIS MORNING AT 9AM, I WAS STANDING ALONE IN MY KITCHEN, DRESSED AND READY TO WALK OUTSIDE AND POWER WALK FOR 30 MINUTES AROUND THE NEIGHBORHOOD.*

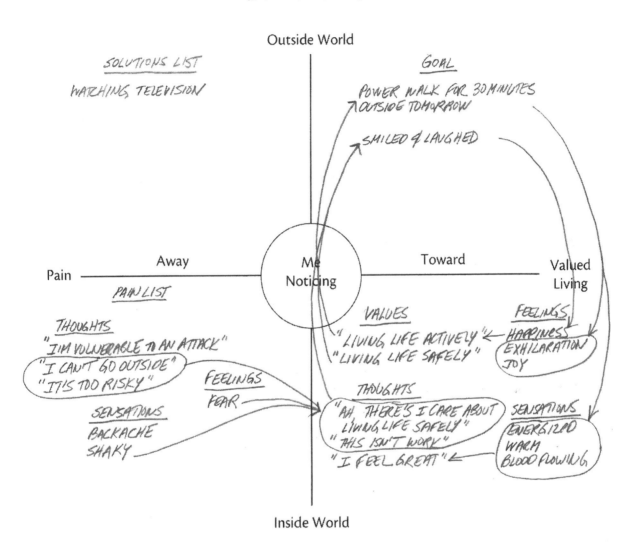

Something to look out for when tracking your actions is whether you're just doing things to feel better or to get or have something instead of doing things in the service of your values. We call this chasing results. For example, imagine you're on patrol with a partner for eight hours (inspired by the Two Kids in the Car metaphor by Russ Harris, 2007). You're driving around focusing on making an arrest and thinking, *When's it going to happen?* For you, it's a shift of frustration just driving around and waiting. Work is all about making an arrest.

Your work partner, on the other hand, is sitting in the other seat and focusing on his values. An arrest would be good, but he's also thinking about *working skillfully and perceptively.*

He's looking out the window at the different cars driving around. He's looking for dirty license plates on clean vehicles, bug-covered license plates on back bumpers, and unlatched trunk lids or tailgates. He's watching what people are doing in cars. Are they moving around a lot or trying to hide things? While driving around, he's listening to different sounds in the neighborhoods. He's doing all these things and appreciating police work while working toward making an arrest.

Now you both reach the location of the arrest. You spot someone trying to break into a house, approach the suspect, talk him into a prone handcuffing position, and handcuff him. You both do a great job and feel good after making the arrest. However, your partner had a rewarding shift. You had a shift of mostly frustration.

When an arrest happens, you'll feel thrilled and successful. But how long do these feelings last? How long before you're looking to make the next arrest? How tiring is it constantly living your life trying to get results? Is this what you do now?_____

_____

_____

_____

Chasing results may also involve thinking or saying things such as "When I feel better, then my life will really start" or "When I feel better, then I can do things again." This when-then thinking puts conditions on achieving your goals, getting results, and experiencing feeling good. What you're actually saying is "I can't do it right now." Feeling good or doing things depends on something else happening in the future. I will feel good or can do things only when these other things happen. Even when you fulfill the conditions, how long does feeling good last? The thing is, chasing results pulls you out of the present situation and into focusing on the future. It means that you can't feel good or do things right now that you can otherwise do and feel by just living your values.

Another thing to be aware of when tracking your actions is whether you do what you say you'll do. It's called the say-do correspondence (Follette & Pistorello, 2007; Rogers-Warren & Baer, 1976). When you begin thinking about changing your behavior and doing something different, your mind may jump the gun. It starts cranking out all sorts of thoughts as if it were a word-generating machine. It tells you things like *I'll fail. I've tried that before. Been there, done that, got the T-shirt. It won't work. It won't matter. Why bother? I'm too anxious. I'm too depressed. I'm too tired. I'll do it later.*

In that moment, such thoughts may sound like perfectly good reasons. So you let your mind tell you what to do and how to feel. You stay put and do the same old thing. You feel guilty for or embarrassed by not keeping your word, which triggers doing more ineffective away moves. Over time, a cycle of saying you'll do something and then not doing it, experiencing pain, and saying you'll do something else that you don't do leads to a lack of say-do correspondence and getting stuck. Is this what you do now?_____

_____

_____

_____

Over time, tracking the consequences of your actions makes it easier to change your behavior. You'll get better at staying on course—noticing when you go off course, changing your direction to get back on course, and learning from your experience. This larger pattern of behavior leads to more valued living (Hayes et al., 1999, 2012; Luoma et al., 2007). A smaller pattern would be just giving up when you fail to achieve a goal the first time. It leads to getting stuck. Occasionally ask people close to you about whether you're living your values. You may ask something like "How would you describe me to a friend or stranger?" What would you hear them say?

_____

_____

_____

_____

_____

_____

_____

One last thing. Don't beat yourself up when you get knocked off course. After all, if beating ourselves up actually worked, then we'd all be perfect by now. The bottom line is to live more fully with purpose and vitality, guided by your values, while you carry your life situations with you.

Before we end with tying together how to continue training up your new skills over the long run, I want to thank you for the opportunity to work with you. Stay safe out there, and thanks for all you do.

How to Practice for Life

Identify some everyday life stories in which painful little things show up and lure you in, and you bite and get hooked. Maybe it's driving in traffic—someone cuts you off or jams on the brakes. Walking through a busy mall, people are walking slowly in front of you and making it difficult or impossible to pass them. Standing in line at the supermarket, the cashier asks for a price check for someone in front of you. Flying on a cross-country flight, the child behind you is crying, and the parents are doing nothing about it.

Perhaps you're sitting in your seat on an airplane, at the gate, after a long flight, and the chime and seat-belt sign goes off, signaling you to get up and exit the plane. However, some passengers behind you jump up, walk toward the exit, and block the aisle. Other passengers are crowding the aisle while getting their bags from the overhead compartments. You're stuck, you can't get out, and you have to wait. What about when driving your car and the passenger is playing back-seat driver, telling you where to go, what to do, and how to drive?

Or how about this one? You're eating dinner with a loved one, on that special date night at your favorite restaurant, but kids are running up and down, yelling, and playing with their food. Their parents are sitting down eating and doing nothing to stop the kids. Another frequent one may be trying to park your car in a busy parking lot. You're waiting for a spot, but someone else pulls into it.

Other ones may be listening to the news, pushing your shopping cart in a busy supermarket, or standing in the screening line at the airport. The list goes on and on. When painful little things show up in these everyday life situations, you can now practice using your new skills so that when big things happen, you're ready. The skills are the same:

1. **Notice it:** Notice painful thoughts and feelings without getting caught up in them.
2. **Stay with it:** Stay with them because on the flip side are usually things you value.
3. **Let it go:** Let go of the habit of moving away from pain.
4. **Choose a direction:** Choose what you value in life.
5. **Just do it:** Take physical action in those chosen life directions.

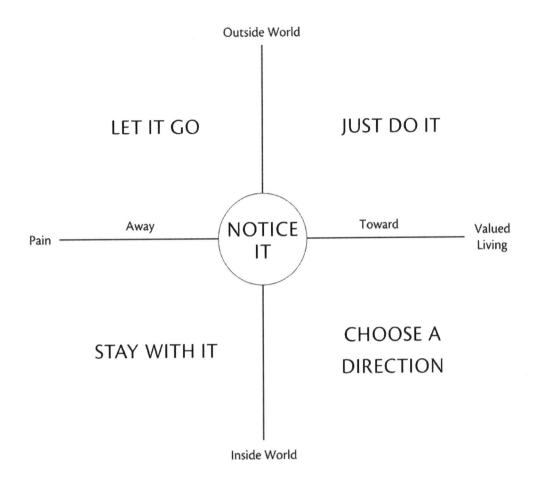

RESOURCES

ACT for Police. Act for Police is the companion website for this book (www.actforpolice.com). You may download all the training worksheets and exercises. There is also much more stuff to help you with training in the skills you've learned here.

Association for Contextual Behavioral Science. The Association for Contextual Behavioral Science is the official website for anyone interested in ACT. You can find an ACT therapist or get self-help information (https://contextualscience.org).

Addictions and Recovery.org. Addictions and Recovery provides recovery information for individuals and families (www.addictionsandrecovery.org).

Smart Recovery. Smart Recovery is a substance abuse and addiction support group in which participants learn recovery tools based on research (www.smartrecovery.org). There are face-to-face meetings, daily online meetings, an online message board, and a 24–7 chat room to obtain recovery support.

Moderation Management. Moderation Management is a behavioral change support group for people concerned about their drinking behavior (www.moderation.org). It leaves the choice of moderation or abstinence up to the individual while promoting self-recognition of risky drinking behavior and healthy lifestyle changes. Face-to-face meetings and online forums are also available to participants.

National Suicide Prevention Lifeline. The National Suicide Prevention Lifeline allows people to get involved in helping others, find a therapist or support group, create a safety plan, watch stories of hope and recovery, learn about mental health and suicide prevention, or speak to someone 24–7 at 1-800-273-8255 (www.suicidepreventionlifeline.org).

Make the Connection. Make the Connection is a resource for veterans, service members, their families and friends, and clinicians (http://maketheconnection.net). However, anyone may use many of the resources available on the website. There is information about behavioral health conditions such as PTSD, depression, or problems with drugs or alcohol. There are also self-help strategies and resources available to support people in recovery. Website visitors may take a brief self-assessment for depression, PTSD, or alcohol or substance abuse to help determine whether it's a good idea to see a professional or to connect with other resources for further assessment and information.

Safe Call Now. Safe Call Now (206-459-3020) is a confidential, comprehensive, twenty-four-hour crisis referral service for public safety employees, emergency services personnel, and their family members nationwide (www.safecallnow.org).

REFERENCES

American Psychiatric Association. (2013). *Diagnostic and statistical manual of mental Disorders: DSM-5* (5th ed.). Arlington, VA: Author.

Childre, D., & Rozman, D. (2005). *Transforming stress: The heartmath solution for relieving worry, fatigue, and tension.* Oakland, CA: New Harbinger.

Chödrön, P. (2002). *The places that scare you: A guide to fearlessness in difficult times.* Boston, MA: Shambhala.

Dahl, J. C., Plumb, J. C., Stewart, I., & Lundgren, T. (2009). *The art & science of valuing in psychotherapy: Helping clients discover, explore, and commit to valued action using acceptance and commitment therapy.* Oakland, CA: New Harbinger.

Dahl, J. C., Wilson, K. G., Luciano, C., & Hayes, S. C. (2005). *Acceptance and commitment therapy for chronic pain.* Reno, NV: Context Press.

Eifert, G. H., & Forsyth, J. P. (2005). *Acceptance and commitment therapy for anxiety disorders: A practitioner's treatment guide to using mindfulness, acceptance, and values-based behavior change strategies.* Oakland, CA: New Harbinger.

Follette, V. M., & Pistorello, J. (2007). *Finding life beyond trauma: Using acceptance and commitment therapy to heal from post-traumatic stress and trauma-related problems.* Oakland, CA. New Harbinger.

Fried, R. L. (1999). *Breathe well, be well: A program to relieve stress, anxiety, asthma, hypertension, migraine, and other disorders for better health.* New York, NY: John Wiley & Sons.

Gallo, F. J. (in press). Police use of force. In J. Kitaeff (Ed.), *Handbook of police psychology* (2nd ed.). New York, NY: Routledge.

Gallo, F. J. (2008). Police occupational socialization. In B. Cutler (Ed.), *Encyclopedia of psychology and law* (Vol. 2, pp. 572–575). Thousand Oaks, CA: Sage.

Gallo, F. J. (2011). Police use of force. In J. Kitaeff (Ed.), *Handbook of police psychology* (pp. 323–343). New York, NY: Routledge.

Harris, R. (2007). *The happiness trap: How to stop struggling and start living: A guide to ACT: The mindfulness-based program for reducing stress, overcoming fear, and creating a rich and meaningful life.* Boston, MA: Trumpeter Books.

Harris, R. (2009). *ACT made simple.* Oakland, CA: New Harbinger.

Hayes, S. C., & Smith, S. (2005). *Get out of your mind and into your life.* Oakland, CA. New Harbinger.

Hayes, S. C., Strosahl, K. D., & Wilson, K. G. (1999). *Acceptance and commitment therapy: An experiential approach to behavior change.* New York, NY: The Guilford Press.

Hayes, S. C., Strosahl, K. D., & Wilson, K. G. (2012). *Acceptance and commitment therapy: The process and practice of mindful change* (2nd ed.). New York, NY: The Guilford Press.

Kessler, R. C., Berglund, P., Demler, O., Jin, R., Merikangas, K. R., & Walters, E. E. (2005). Lifetime prevalence and age-of-onset distributions of DSM-IV disorders in the National Comorbidity Survey Replication. *Archives of General Psychiatry, 62*(6), 593–602.

Klinger, D. (2002). *Police responses to officer-involved shootings* (Report No. 192286). Retrieved from the National Criminal Justice Reference Service website: www.ncjrs.gov/pdffiles1/nij/grants/192286.pdf.

Lehrer, P. M., Vaschillo, E. G., & Vaschillo B. (2000). Resonant frequency biofeedback training to increase cardiac variability: Rationale and manual for training. *Applied Psychophysiology and Biofeedback, 25*(3), 177–191.

Levine, P. A. (2008). *Healing trauma: A pioneering program for restoring the wisdom of your body.* Boulder, CO: Sounds True.

Litz, B. T., Stein, N., Delaney, E., Lebowitz, L., Nash, W. P., Silva, C., & Maguen, S. (2009). Moral injury and moral repair in war veterans: A preliminary model and intervention strategy. *Clinical Psychology Review, 29*(8), 695–706.

Luoma, J. B., Hayes, S. C., & Walser, R. D. (2007). *Learning ACT: An acceptance & commitment therapy skills-training manual for therapists.* Oakland, CA: New Harbinger.

Maguen, S., Metzler, T. J., Litz, B. T., Seal, K. H., Knight, S. J., & Marmar, C. R. (2009). The impact of killing in war on mental health symptoms and related functioning. *Journal of Traumatic Stress, 22*(5), 435–443.

Maguen, S., Vogt, D. S., King, L. A., King, D. W., Litz, B. T., Knight, S. J., & Marmar, C. R. (2011). The impact of killing on mental health symptoms in Gulf War veterans. *Psychological Trauma: Theory, Research, Practice, and Policy, 3*(1), 21–26.

Nilsson, S., Hyllengren, P., Ohlsson, A., Kallenberg, K., Waaler, G., & Larsson, G. (2015). Leadership and moral stress: Individual reaction patterns among first responders in acute situations that involve moral stressors. *Journal of Trauma & Treatment, S4.* doi:10.4172/2167-1222.S4-025.

Polk, K. (2011). *Psychological flexibility training (PFT): Flexing your mind along with your muscles.* Seattle, WA: Amazon Digital Services.

Polk, K., Schoendorff, B., Webster, M., & Olaz, F. O. (2016). *The essential guide to the ACT Matrix: A step-by-step approach to using the ACT Matrix model in clinical practice.* Oakland, CA: Context Press.

Riskind, J. H. (1997). Looming vulnerability to threat: A cognitive paradigm for anxiety. *Behavior Research and Therapy, 35*(8), 685–702.

Rogers-Warren, A., & Baer, D. M. (1976). Correspondence between saying and doing: Teaching children to share and praise. *Journal of Applied Behavior Analysis, 9*(3), 335–354.

Stoddard, J. A., & Afari, N. (2014). *The big book of ACT metaphors: A practitioner's guide to experiential exercises & metaphors in acceptance and commitment therapy.* Oakland, CA: New Harbinger.

Vaschillo, E. G., Lehrer, P., Rishe, N., & Konstantinov, M. (2002). Heart rate variability biofeedback as a method for addressing baroflex function: A preliminary study of resonance in the cardiovascular system. *Human Physiology, 9,* 257–265.

Vaschillo, E. G., Vaschillo, B., & Lehrer, P. M. (2006). Characteristics of resonance in heart rate variability stimulated by biofeedback. *Applied Psychophysiology and Biofeedback, 31*(2), 129–142.

Walser, R. D., & Westrup, D. (2007). *Acceptance and commitment therapy for the treatment of post-traumatic stress disorder & trauma-related problems: A practitioner's guide to using mindfulness & acceptance strategies.* Oakland, CA: New Harbinger.

Made in the USA
Middletown, DE
13 August 2017